D0881567

QUEST Program II

Social Skills Curriculum for Middle School Students with Autism

Ready-to-use lessons with games,
role-play activities, and more!

QUEST Program II was developed by

JoEllen Cumpata, MA, CCC
Speech and Language Pathologist

Susan Fell, LMSW
Student Assistance Specialist

QUEST Program II: Social Skills Curriculum for Middle School Students with Autism

All marketing and publishing rights guaranteed to and reserved by

721 W. Abram Street
Arlington, Texas 76013
800-489-0727
817-277-0727
817-277-2270 (fax)
E-mail: info@FHautism.com
www.FHautism.com

Printed in United States of America

Publisher's Cataloging-In-Publication Data

(Prepared by The Donohue Group, Inc.)

Cumpata, JoEllen. QUEST Program II: Social Skills Curriculum for Middle School Students with Autism / developed by JoEllen Cumpata [and] Susan Fell.

   p. : ill. ; cm. + 1 CD.

   Accompanied by a CD containing lessons, worksheets, and visual aids from the book in PDF format.

   "The QUEST Program II was developed by JoEllen Cumpata, Susan Fell."

   Includes bibliographical references and index.   ISBN: 9781941765098

1. Social skills in children--Study and teaching. 2. Autisistic children--Education. 3. Asperger's syndrome--Patients--Education. 4. Developmentally disabled children--Education. 5. Inclusive education. I. Fell, Susan. II. Title.

LC4717.5 .C86 2010
371.92

ISBN: 9781941765098

To our students,
who continue to inspire us
with their wit, humor, and courage.

About the Authors

JoEllen Cumpata is currently a school-based Speech Language Pathologist (SLP). She was formerly a clinical supervisor at Michigan State University, teaching classes related to providing school-based speech and language services. JoEllen also served as a clinical SLP at Massachusetts General Hospital and Children's Hospital of Boston, working with adults and children. JoEllen has a Master's degree in Speech Language Pathology.

Susan Fell has been a school social worker for 15 years working primarily at the middle school level with students with autism, emotional, and cognitive impairments. Prior to that, Susan was a vocational counselor, youth employment coordinator, and parenting educator. She earned her Master's degree in Social Work from Arizona State University and her School Social Work Certification from Wayne State University in Detroit, Michigan.

The authors welcome your feedback! You can e-mail them at QUESTsocialskills@gmail.com.

Table of Contents

Sections marked with ⬤ are also included on the companion CD-ROM.

FAQs

What does QUEST stand for?

QUEST stands for **Q**uestioning, **U**nderstanding, and **E**xploring **S**ocial Skills and Pragmatic Language **T**ogether.

Why was QUEST Program II created?

QUEST Program II was created to help middle school students on the autism spectrum who experience challenges in the areas of social skills and pragmatic language.

What is QUEST Program II?

- QUEST Program II is a school-based social skills program.

- Units were selected to target skills most needed by middle school students.

  1. School Survival Basics

  2. Understanding and Managing Emotions

  3. Communication Skills

  4. Making Friends and Interacting With Peers

  5. Personal Safety

  6. Vocational Readiness

Where and how often do groups meet?

- Students enrolled in QUEST Program II meet in a middle school classroom two to three times weekly for 45 minutes.

- Students are seated in a circular fashion.

- Important visual cues direct activities.

- Supplies are readily available.

How are QUEST Program II skills taught?

- Predictable weekly schedule

- Routine daily procedures

- Sequential experiential stories

- Hands-on activities, games, and practice

- Poster boards

- Classroom presentations and feedback

- Incentives

- Regular parent e-mail updates

- Parent and teacher evaluation of student progress

Why start a social skills program?

The QUEST Program II question is not *why*, but *why not!*

See the opposite page for a list of common challenges associated with starting a social skills program, along with how to remedy them.

Challenges	Misconceptions	What We Have Learned	Benefits
Scheduling	There is not enough time to meet several times weekly with students.	Placing students in groups reduces the need for individual meetings and can be a much more effective use of time.	Intensive, sequential, and repetitive instruction increases chances of generalization.
Academic Priorities	Academic instruction is more important that social skills instruction.	Parents and teachers quickly observe and appreciate the results of intensive social skills instruction, and priorities change. Parents and teams need to work together to determine what is best for each child.	Intensive social skills instruction improves classroom and home behavior and increases academic success.
Staffing	A program of this magnitude requires heavy staffing.	While an optimum program would utilize two full-time staff several times weekly, it could be facilitated by one person and meet as little as twice weekly and still be effective.	Social Workers, Speech Pathologists, and teachers regularly work on these goals with students. Combining efforts and teaching in groups maximizes effectiveness in a shorter period of time.
Funding	A program of this magnitude requires large sums of money.	Keeping costs low is the result of planning and creativity. Supplies needed are inexpensive. Games and poster boards are easy to create.	Games and poster boards are reusable, and can easily be updated.
Perfectionism	We need to find the perfect program before we can begin.	Developing and refining a social skills program takes time. Just get started; your program will improve with age!	Providing students with opportunities for regular social skills practice is beneficial. Even if this means focusing on only one or two skills each year.

About QUEST Program II

The QUEST Program II Story

QUEST Program II was developed by a school social worker and speech language pathologist to address the needs of children with autism and Asperger's syndrome (AS). The program uses an intensive proactive approach to teaching social skills, combining written instruction with games, activities, and student interaction. The goal of the program is to help students gain a better understanding of human behavior and interaction, and to provide them with opportunities to become familiar and comfortable with the social skills and pragmatic language necessary to be successful at school and in the community.

Students with social skills deficits benefit from regular instruction and practice in order to maximize generalization of skills outside of the classroom. Unlike their peers, these students do not typically interpret social cues, nuances, and rules of interaction, even when provided with an inclusive education in a general education setting. Often adolescents with autism or AS begin to recognize this difference, and can easily become overwhelmed or anxious around their peers. QUEST Program II students learn about social skills through experiential stories, role play, games, activities, discussion, friendly feedback from peers, and real-world experience.

Supportive Research

QUEST Program II provides systematic instruction in social skills and pragmatic language development. The program is based on a body of research which suggests that social relationships are a key component of success in individuals with Asperger's syndrome (AS) (Tantam, 1991). Researchers Gresham, Sugai and Horner (2001) reported that "the ability to interact successfully with peers and significant others is one of the most important areas of students' development."

Treatment of social skills deficits is a well documented intervention for children with AS (Attwood, 1998; 2000; 2003; Bock, 2001; and Klin, Sparrow, Marans, Carter, & Volkmar, 2000). Clinical expertise, paired with evidence from credible research, suggests that social skills training can be considered an evidence-based practice (ASHA Position Statement, 2005).

Empirical data suggests that the most effective social skills training for students with developmental disabilities such as AS incorporate modeling, coaching, and reinforcement systems. Additionally, while generalization and maintenance have traditionally been the weak links in social skills training programs, they are considered crucial parts of this type of programming (Gresham et al. 2001).

With these factors in mind, the QUEST Program II curriculum was designed to teach the "hidden curriculum" and unwritten rules of social interaction. In order to address social, emotional, and pragmatic language learning, QUEST Program II training is provided in units. The program provides intensive, sequential instruction in an interactive format that appeals to adolescents. Generalization and maintenance of learned skills are emphasized.

Program Description

QUEST Program II consists of six units covering a variety of topics, including School Survival Basics, Understanding and Managing Emotions, Communication Skills, Making Friends and Interacting with Peers, Personal Safety, and Vocational Readiness. Topics can be presented at home with parents or other family members, or in a small group or classroom setting. The program was designed to be co-taught in a school setting, but it can be adapted for use by parents, therapists, or others.

Each topic is presented during a three-class cycle; however, activity days can be lengthened or modified as needed. Day one provides students with basic information about the skill by reading and discussing an experiential story. Day two gives students the opportunity to practice the skill through individual and group activities, including investigation, observation, group projects, games, and role play. Day three reinforces learning as students work together in a small group to compile and present a report highlighting their understanding of the skill. Students are reminded of and expected to use learned skills during subsequent lessons.

It is highly recommended that QUEST Program II students meet two to three times per week for approximately 45 minutes. Group size is most effective when limited to eight students. Facilitators utilize a predictable schedule, visual reminders, regular prompts and feedback regarding learned skills, and reinforcers to maximize learning. Students benefit from working in a team while learning about behaviors, demonstrating understanding, and practicing in a safe environment. Weekly updates with suggestions for continued practice at home are provided to parents. Skill generalization is evaluated by both parents and teachers upon completion of each unit.

Weekly Schedule

Following a predictable weekly schedule helps reduce student anxiety. An organized classroom with a supply closet containing individual QUEST Program II binders, materials, and snacks is helpful. Students are expected to report to class on time and complete check-in procedures daily. These procedures can be varied, but typically include gathering materials and writing the day's topic in a planner. Colorful "QUEST Program II Rules and Procedures" posters and daily activity reminder cards are displayed in the classroom to help students remember procedures and successfully meet expectations. The date and current topic should also be written clearly on the board.

Activities

Each experiential story is supported by one or more activities. Procedures and materials needed are described on activity sheets. Activities may involve role-play, use of scenario cards, laminated poster boards, or handouts.

Materials for each activity are included and will need to be copied on colored paper or card stock before use. It is recommended that they be laminated if possible, and some materials may need to be enlarged and placed on poster boards if used in a group setting. Encouraging students to move about, role-play, or interact during activities increases interest and learning.

Activities are designed to help students become comfortable with skills and generalize learning. Each may be repeated throughout the year and facilitators and parents should encourage continued skill use.

Reinforcement

Students with social and pragmatic language skill deficits may not understand the importance or need for social skill instruction and practice. Often these students are unaware of their deficits and may be reluctant to participate in the program. Providing incentives is one way to encourage participation. Additionally, students benefit from feedback from teachers, facilitators, parents, and peers.

Incentive guidelines are presented to students during the first week of class. Tickets, tokens, or coupons can be used as a motivational tool to encourage students to complete basic classroom procedures. Criteria for earning incentives should be concrete and achievable. Suggested criteria include arriving to class on time, completing check-in procedures, and participating in discussion or activities. Tokens can also be combined for group-earned activities such as a movie or pizza day.

Parent Support

Gaining parental and academic team support is essential to program success. Parent updates provide parents with information and suggestions to assist them in continuing to practice at home. Sample Parent Updates, fliers, evaluations, and additional information are included for your use.

Parent Updates

QUEST Program II Parent Updates are designed to enable parents to continue skill-building at home with their child. Each experiential story can be supported with a Parent Update, which can be e-mailed or sent home to parents. Specific guidelines are given in each update to assist parents in understanding what skill has been taught, specific rules or vocabulary used to support the skill, and ways to practice at home.

Student Evaluation

Student evaluations can be provided to parents, teachers, or others to determine if skills are becoming generalized. Evaluation can also be used as a pre/post assessment.

Unit Descriptions

Advanced topics are included for use with second or third year students and are indicated with an "A."

Unit 1 –School Survival Basics

- Greetings
- Paying Attention
- Daily Hygiene
- Asking for Help
- Creating a Workspace and Completing Work

Unit 2 – Understanding and Managing Emotions

- Understanding Feelings
- Uncomfortable Feelings
- Getting Angry/Calming Down
- Managing Stress
- Negotiating with Others – A
- Problem Solving – A

Unit 3 – Communication Skills

- Nonverbal Communication
- Starting a Conversation
- Keeping a Conversation Going
- Ending a Conversation
- Joining a Group Conversation – A
- Exiting an Uncomfortable Conversation – A

Unit 4 – Making Friends and Interacting with Peers

- Friends are Important
- Making and Keeping Friends
- Making Plans with Friends
- Using the Telephone
- Modesty
- Recognizing and Dealing with Gossiping, Bullying, and Teasing
- Resisting Peer Pressure – A
- Participating in After-School Activities – A
- Dating – A

Unit 5 – Personal Safety

- Being Home Alone
- Using the Telephone in an Emergency
- Smoke and Fire Alarm Safety
- Being Separated from My Group
- Internet and E-mail Safety – A
- Driving with Friends – A
- Drugs, Alcohol, and Dangerous Behavior – A

Unit 6 – Vocational Readiness

- My Skills and Interests – A
- Working for Others – A
- Creating a Flier and Applying for a Summer Job – A
- Accepting Suggestions and Compliments from My Employer - A

QUEST Program II: Social Skills Curriculum for Middle School Students with Autism
© by JoEllen Cumpata and Susan Fell. Future Horizons, Inc.

Sample Correspondence, Reports, and Forms

On the following pages you will find samples of the correspondence and forms used in QUEST.

Form 1   Teacher Introductory Flier – to present program to teachers and other administrative and support staff.

Form 2   Parent Introductory Letter – to inform parents when their child has been identified as a possible candidate for QUEST.

Form 3   Parent Introductory Flier (two samples provided) – to present program to parents of students who may be eligible for participation in the program or for students already enrolled.

Form 4   QUEST Program II Parent/Teacher Evaluation – to inform parents and teachers of skills

recently learned and gain feedback on generalization of skills.

Form 5   QUEST Program II Rules and Procedures – visual reminder to display in the classroom.

Form 6   Daily Reminder Cards – visual reminders to display in the classroom.

Form 7   Student Group Report – weekly report form completed by students.

Form 8   Pre/Post Assessment – given to students prior to program and again upon completion. Note: pre/post test is designed for use with all six QUEST Program II units.

QUEST Program II is now available for students who may benefit from direct instruction and support for improving social and pragmatic language skills. Students participate two days per week in lieu of their academic assistance, skills, or prevocational classes. The class is facilitated by a teacher, speech pathologist, school social worker, or psychologist. Parent permission is required.

QUEST Program II

Questioning, Understanding, and Exploring Social Skills and Pragmatic Language Together

The goals of QUEST Program II are to improve student social and pragmatic language skills through use of experiential stories, small group work, role play, games, activities, and regular practice. Topics covered include:

- School Survival Basics
- Understanding and Managing Emotions
- Communication Skills
- Making Friends and Interacting with Peers
- Personal Safety
- Vocational Readiness

Parents are given suggestions on ways they can assist in reinforcing and maintaining skill development. Teachers and parents may also be asked to provide monthly feedback regarding progress.

If you have questions or would like a program facilitator to share information with parents and the team at the next IEP, please complete the form attached and return to:

_____.

- -

QUEST Program II Student Nomination Form

Student Name _____ Grade_____

Nominator's Name/Phone_____

Next IEP Date _____ School_____

(School Letterhead)

(Date)

Dear (parent name),

(School name) currently offers the QUEST Program II program for students who may benefit from additional opportunities during the school day to learn and practice nonverbal and social interaction. Your child has been identified as someone who may gain valuable skills from participation in this program.

Classes are scheduled in lieu of your child's "Skills" or "Prevocational" period and meet two days per week. Students participate in a small-group setting and have opportunities for hands-on practice, role play, and other experiential activities designed to increase their proficiency and comfort with appropriate social skills.

Enclosed you will find a flier describing the program. Please contact your child's special education teacher if you have questions or wish to discuss the program in detail.

Sincerely,

Welcome to Student QUEST Program II

Students Questioning, Understanding, and Exploring Social Skills and Pragmatic Language Together

Your student is scheduled to participate in the Student QUEST Program II program this year.

- The goals of this program are to improve student social interaction and communication skills through the use of experiential stories, small group work, role-plays, hands-on activities, and regular practice.

- Students meet in a small-group setting two days each week during their skill period.

- Please see the list of the topics we will be covering this year.

- Weekly updates will be e-mailed to parents, with helpful suggestions on ways you can support your child's success.

The Student QUEST Program II facilitators are:

_____

_____

_____

QUEST Program II

Questioning, Understanding, and Exploring Social Skills and Pragmatic Language Together

Does your child need additional support to ...

- make and keep friends?

- interpret body language and other social cues?

- manage emotions and handle stress?

If so, they may benefit from participation in QUEST Program II

- The goals of this program are to improve student social interaction and communication skills through the use of experiential stories, small-group work, role-plays, hands-on activities, and regular practice.

- Students meet in a small-group setting twice per week.

- Weekly updates are e-mailed to parents, and provide helpful suggestions on concrete ways to maintain and build skills at home.

- QUEST Program II is offered for _____ grade students with more in-depth study and advanced topics presented to second and third year participants. Units include:

    1. School Survival Basics

    2. Understanding and Managing Emotions

    3. Communication Skills

    4. Making Friends and Interacting with Peers

    5. Personal Safety

    6. Vocational Readiness

For more information contact: _____

QUEST Program II Parent/Teacher Evaluation

Student Name _____ Date _____

Parent/Teacher Name _____

The past several weeks in QUEST Program II we have been focusing on:

_____

Please complete the rating scale below to assist us in determining how well the student listed above has generalized the skills taught. Check boxes that identify how often you have observed the skills listed during the past few weeks.

How often observed

Skill	Often	Sometimes	Never

Comments _____

_____

_____

Thank you for your input!

Classroom Rules and Procedures

Students participating in QUEST Program II are expected to follow standard rules and procedures. Rules help students feel comfortable and help teachers maintain an efficient classroom.

1. Come to QUEST Program II on time.

2. Come to QUEST Program II without complaining.

3. Complete "check-in" procedures.
   - Complete your planner
   - Get your binder
   - Have a seat

4. Participate in daily activities.
   - Pay attention
   - Answer questions
   - Complete activities
   - Present group reports

Story Day —————→ Learn

Activity Day —————→ Practice

Report Day —————→ Share

QUEST Program II Student Group Report

Names _____

Date _____ Skill we are learning about _____

This is the way we learned about this skill:

_____ Read a story about the skill

_____ Demonstrated or watched others demonstrate the skill

_____ Used cards

_____ Used a poster board game

_____ Other _____

This is what we learned:

Learning about this skill is important because

_____

Two things we need to remember when we use this skill are

_____

One mistake students can make when they use this skill is

_____

We can practice this skill by

_____

QUEST Program II Pre/Post Assessment

Name _____ Date _____

Answer each question or fill in the blanks.

1. One way to greet a student in the hall is to

   _____

2. Teachers know that you are paying attention when you

   _____

3. One thing students can do every day to maintain good hygiene is

   _____

4. I can look at someone's face or body and tell when they are angry because they

   _____

5. One way I can relax when I feel stress is

   _____

6. It is important to greet other students because

   _____

7.   Something I have in common with other students is

_____

8.   When I talk with another person, I should stand an _____

away so we both feel comfortable.

9.   When students are talking we say it is like Ping-Pong because they

_____

10.   Two things I should do before I can call another student on the telephone are

_____

11.   One thing students can do to have fun together after school is

_____

12.   Students may experience peer pressure in school. One example of peer pressure is

_____

13.   The telephone number I can call in an emergency at home is

_____

14.   I should not share personal information with strangers. One example of "personal

information" is my _____

15.   If I get confused when I am away from home I can find a helpful person.

One place I can usually find a helpful person is standing near a

_____

16.   Two things students can do when they feel uncomfortable emotions are

_____

17.   It is important for my family to have a fire-safety plan because

_____

18.   Secondary students do not hug their school principal, the mailman, or strangers.

One person students may hug is their

_____

19.   One thing I can put in my homework space is a

_____

20.   Looking at someone when they are talking to you is called

_____

Unit 1

School Survival Basics

Goal

To learn and practice basic skills needed to function successfully in school

Objectives

- ➤ To understand and use informal greetings at school and home.

- ➤ To realize the importance of and practice being attentive in class and during conversation.

- ➤ To learn about puberty and basic adolescent hygiene.

- ➤ To gain a level of comfort when seeking the help of an adult.

- ➤ To understand the importance of completing work, and create an environment at home and school conducive to study.

- ➤ To learn and practice basic organizational skills, including utilizing the school assignment book, coming to class prepared, and organizing daily materials for each class.

Experiential Stories, Activities, and Parent Updates

Stories can be read by parents, teachers, or students. Often students gain a deeper understanding of skills when stories can be discussed in detail in a group setting. Asking students to summarize paragraphs, relate their personal experiences, and complete activities are all effective ways to increase generalization of skills. Parent Updates provide additional ways to continue learning at home.

Topics included in this unit are:

1. Greetings

2. Paying Attention

3. Daily Hygiene

4. Asking for Help

5. Creating a Workspace and Completing Work

6. Organizing Work and Using an Assignment Book

Greetings – Experiential Story

When I am at home, in school, or in my community, it is nice to be friendly. One way students can be friendly at school is by greeting each other. When students greet each other or an adult at school, they are being friendly. If students do not use greetings, people might think that they do not want to be friendly.

There are many ways to greet people at school. Sometimes students need to be quiet, like in class or in the library. Students can use a silent greeting by smiling or waving at a person. When a student smiles or waves, it is important that the other person is looking at them.

In the halls or during lunch at school, or in the community, students can say, "Hello!," "Hi," or "How are you?" when they greet one another. Sometimes students even use interesting or creative greetings like, "What up?" or "Hey." Students may also use names when greeting each other, like, "Hey Jim, how are you?"

When students use a greeting, they usually look at the face of the person they are greeting and smile. It is important that students wait until they are about an arm's length from another person before greeting them with words. When students are about an arm's length away, and they are smiling and looking at the face of the other person, they can say, "Hi," or "Hello," and be heard.

If students are meeting an adult for the first time, or greeting someone important like a teacher, the principal or vice principal, or a guest speaker, they can shake hands. This lets the person know that you respect them and are happy to see them. Usually students don't shake hands with each other in school. Shaking hands is a greeting for adults and important people.

At home, students may greet their family and relatives with a hug or a kiss. Hugs and kisses are only for people we love, usually family, relatives, and close friends. In school, students do not usually hug teachers or other students. Sometimes if close friends are excited and happy to see each other outside of school they may hug each other. It is inappropriate for students to kiss each other at school.

I can be friendly and use greetings at school. I can wave or smile at other students in class and in the library. Before I greet a student I can remember to look at them, smile, and move about one arm's length away so I will be heard. I can say, "Hello," "Hi," or "How are you?" when I see students I know in the halls or at lunch. I can also greet people I do not know if I want to become their friend. I can shake hands with important adults, or people I am meeting for the first time. At home I can hug and kiss people I love in order to greet them. Using greetings lets people know that I am a friendly person.

QUEST Program II: Social Skills Curriculum for Middle School Students with Autism
© by JoEllen Cumpata and Susan Fell. Future Horizons, Inc.

Greetings – Activity Sheet

Materials

- ❑ "Greetings" experiential story
- ❑ Greetings Flash Cards handout
- ❑ Magazines
- ❑ Scissors
- ❑ Glue Sticks

Procedure

- ❑ Read the "Greetings" experiential story.
- ❑ Look through magazines to find pictures of people smiling, waving, and shaking hands.
- ❑ Cut out pictures and paste in appropriate location on the Greetings Flash Cards handout.
- ❑ Students share with the group.
- ❑ Cut out cards to use for role-play activity.

Greetings Flash Cards

Greetings are ways people can be friendly. We can greet each other in many ways. Find pictures in magazines to illustrate each greeting below, and then create your own flash cards.

Smiling	Waving

Shaking Hands	Giving a Hug or Kiss

QUEST Program II: Social Skills Curriculum for Middle School Students with Autism
© by JoEllen Cumpata and Susan Fell. Future Horizons, Inc.

Greetings Role-Plays – Activity Sheet

Materials

- ❑ "Greetings" experiential story
- ❑ Greetings flash cards (cut into cards after first activity)
- ❑ Greeting Role-Play cards

Procedure

- ❑ Read the "Greetings" experiential story.
- ❑ Ask one student to hold up the first Greetings flash card and read it.
- ❑ Discuss when it is appropriate to smile, use a verbal greeting, wave, and hug.
- ❑ Have students draw Greetings Role-Play cards and practice appropriate greetings for each.

Greetings Role-Play cards

Directions: Copy on colored paper, laminate, and cut into cards.

Walking down the hall at school.

Meeting your mom's boss.

Greeting your grandparents at the family reunion.

Seeing a friend at the grocery store.

Passing a friend in the library.

Meeting a friend on the playground.

Seeing someone you know at a movie theater.

Greeting your teacher before class.

QUEST Program II: Social Skills Curriculum for Middle School Students with Autism
© by JoEllen Cumpata and Susan Fell. Future Horizons, Inc.

Greeting the principal at school.

Greeting a teacher in the hall.

Greeting a teacher on the playground.

Seeing someone you know at church.

Seeing someone you know across the room in math class.

Greeting your dad when he returns home from work.

Welcoming your aunt when she comes to visit.

Welcoming your cousin at Thanksgiving.

Meeting the President of the United States.

Seeing the assistant principal across the gym at a school dance.

Meeting a famous singer.

Greeting a salesman who comes to your door.

Passing someone on the street who you do not know.

Passing someone at the mall who you do not know.

Walking past a neighbor on your way home from school.

Walking past the mailman on your way home from school.

QUEST Program II: Social Skills Curriculum for Middle School Students with Autism
© by JoEllen Cumpata and Susan Fell. Future Horizons, Inc.

QUEST Program II UPDATE!

Dear Parent,

This week your child has been working hard in QUEST Program II to master the skill of

Using Greetings

Together we have learned and practiced:

- Why people use greetings—to be friendly.

- Things to remember before you greet someone—hold your head up, smile, look at the person and stand about one arm's length away.

- Which greetings to use

  1. Say, "Hi," "Hello," or "How are you?" to friends at school or in the community.

  2. Wave when someone is far away or in a quiet place.

  3. Shake hands with important people and grown-ups.

  4. Hug and kiss family members and loved ones. (We encourage our students to discuss this with parents if it feels uncomfortable. It is not uncommon for adolescents to become uneasy with displays of affection.)

You can reinforce the learning at home by:

- Discussing which greeting they would use in different situations, e.g., "If we see Mrs. Smith today at the grocery store, how should we greet her?"

- Praising them for using appropriate greetings, e.g., "I noticed that when you said hello to Dr. Stevens you looked right at his face and smiled. I'm sure he thought you were a friendly young man."

- Reminding them to greet others when they forget, e.g., "I see Carolyn looking at you from across the room. Why don't you wave at her to let her know you see her, too?"

- Noticing if your child appears uncomfortable with affectionate responses from adults, and discussing ways to handle the situation, e.g., "I noticed you rubbed your cheek when Aunt Sylvia kissed you. How about if next time you put out your hand and ask her to shake?"

Thanks for your help!

Paying Attention – Experiential Story

At school, students learn about many different things. In class, teachers give information, talk about rules, assign homework and projects, and sometimes even tell jokes. Sometimes teachers give interesting information. Sometimes the information is boring.

Students also talk to other students in school. Sometimes students are up in front of the class giving a presentation. Other times students talk to one another in a small group while working on a class assignment. Students also talk to one another in the halls, at lunch, and outside of school.

When someone is talking, it is important to pay attention. If students do not pay attention, they might not hear something important. Teachers expect that all students will pay attention when the teacher is talking in class. Other students expect that their friends and fellow students will pay attention when they are talking. Teachers and friends might think students are being rude if they don't pay attention during discussions or conversations.

Looking like we are paying attention during classroom instruction, discussions, or when we are having conversation with friends is important. If students do not look like they are paying attention, people might think that they are not interested, that they are not learning, or that they don't care about what is being said. If we don't pay attention, others might think we are being rude. People know we are paying attention to them when we

- Look at their face when they are talking.

- Keep our back and shoulders straight.

- Keep our hands and feet still.

- Listen and don't talk.

- Wait until the person stops talking to raise our hand, make a comment, or ask questions.

It is important to pay attention, even if the person talking is boring. Some students can listen with their eyes closed, their head down, or when they are doing something else. It is important to look like we are paying attention even if we can listen with our head down, or with our eyes looking elsewhere. When we look like we are paying attention, others know that they are being heard and we are being polite.

I can pay attention to people when they are talking to me. I can try to look like I am paying attention even when the other person is boring. I can look at their face, keep my back and shoulders straight, keep my hands and feet still, listen, and wait to talk until the other person is

QUEST Program II: Social Skills Curriculum for Middle School Students with Autism
© by JoEllen Cumpata and Susan Fell. Future Horizons, Inc.

finished talking. When I pay attention, people know I am interested and that I have heard everything they are saying. When I look like I am paying attention, people think I am being polite.

Paying Attention – Activity Sheet

Materials

- ❏ "Paying Attention" experiential story
- ❏ Paying Attention Flash Cards handout
- ❏ Magazines
- ❏ Scissors
- ❏ Glue Stick

Procedure

- ❏ Read the "Paying Attention" experiential story.
- ❏ Look through magazines to find pictures of people paying attention.
- ❏ Cut out pictures and paste in appropriate location on Paying Attention Flash Cards handout.
- ❏ Students share with the group.

Alternate Activity

Have students create a mural with magazine cutouts. One side of the mural should show people paying attention. The other side should show people who are not paying attention. Ask students to share their murals during report time.

Paying Attention Flash Cards

When people pay attention, they use good eye contact, keep their head up and their back straight, and keep their hands and feet still. Find pictures of people who are and are not paying attention and glue in the appropriate boxes below.

People who are paying attention look like this

People who are NOT paying attention look like this

QUEST Program II: Social Skills Curriculum for Middle School Students with Autism
© by JoEllen Cumpata and Susan Fell. Future Horizons, Inc.

Paying Attention - Activity Sheet

Materials

- ❑ "Paying Attention" experiential story
- ❑ Paying Attention flash cards (cut from handout on last activity)

Procedure

- ❑ Read the "Paying Attention" experiential story.
- ❑ Ask student to get out their Paying Attention and Not Paying Attention flash cards.
- ❑ Tell students you will be demonstrating a behavior and they are to hold up their Paying Attention card if they believe you are paying attention, or their Not Paying Attention card if they feel you are not paying attention.
- ❑ Tell students you will now be playing the "Paying Attention-Not Paying Attention game."
- ❑ Instruct the class to "Not pay attention." Encourage students to move about, make noise, etc.
- ❑ Give the direction, "Class, pay attention."
- ❑ The last student to comply is "out."
- ❑ Repeat asking students to not pay attention, and pay attention until one student remains and is the winner.
- ❑ Students who are "out" can observe the others and assist in noticing who is first and last to comply with directions.

Alternate Activities

- ❑ Have students draw cards and demonstrate behaviors.
- ❑ Ask students to role-play "Paying Attention" or "Not Paying Attention."
- ❑ Have others determine which they are acting out and explain how they knew.

Paying Attention - Activity Sheet

Materials

- ❑ "Paying Attention" experiential story
- ❑ Paying Attention/Not Paying Attention cards
- ❑ Paying Attention Body Language cards

Procedure

- ❑ Read the "Paying Attention" experiential story.
- ❑ Hand out set of Paying Attention/Not Paying Attention cards to each student.
- ❑ Place Paying Attention Body Language cards upside down on the table.
- ❑ Ask students to choose one Body Language card and demonstrate it for the group
- ❑ Tell the group they are to hold up their Paying Attention card if the student appears to be paying attention, or their Not Paying Attention card if the student does not appear to be paying attention.

Paying Attention/Not Paying Attention cards

Directions: Copy on colored paper, laminate, and cut into cards.

Paying Attention	Not Paying Attention

Paying Attention Body Language cards

Directions: Copy on colored paper, laminate, and cut into cards.

Head up	**Mouth smiling**
Head down	**Mouth frowning**
Back straight	**Body still**

Back bent	Body moving
Eyes wide open	Arms crossed
Nodding	Fingers tapping
Raising hand	Legs/knees bouncing

QUEST Program II: Social Skills Curriculum for Middle School Students with Autism
© by JoEllen Cumpata and Susan Fell. Future Horizons, Inc.

Slouching

Sitting up straight

Talking to others

Asking questions

QUEST Program II UPDATE!

Dear Parent,

This week your child has been working hard in QUEST Program II to master the skill of

Paying Attention

Together we have learned and practiced:

- Why it is important to pay attention, even if the person speaking is boring. (Ask your child why.)

- How learning to pay attention can help students get better grades.

- How it looks when someone is paying attention:

   1. Looking at the speaker's face

   2. Sitting or standing with a straight back

   3. Stopping talking, and listening

   4. Keeping hands/feet still

You can reinforce the learning at home by:

- Reminding your child to "pay attention" when you speak to them.

- Being a good role model and giving your child your full attention when they speak with you. It is important for parents to validate their children. If children try to talk to you at a bad time say, "Honey, this seems very important to you, but I'm in the middle of … Could we talk about this after dinner when I can give you my full attention?"

- Making sure your child is looking at your face and that they have stopped moving and talking before you begin to talk.

- Praising them when you notice good attention, e.g., "I know you've heard Grandpa tell that story before, but you gave him your full attention. It was a very polite thing to do." "Thank you for listening to all my ideas. You paid great attention. Now I want to hear how you would like to do it."

Thanks for your help!

QUEST Program II: Social Skills Curriculum for Middle School Students with Autism
© by JoEllen Cumpata and Susan Fell. Future Horizons, Inc.

Daily Hygiene – Experiential Story

Parents are responsible for taking care of small children. When students get older, it is important that they start becoming responsible for themselves, and especially maintaining proper hygiene. This means dressing neatly and looking clean, smelling good, and making sure their body is healthy.

Student's bodies are going through many changes. They are becoming adults. It is normal for students to sweat under their arms when it is hot or when they move around a lot. Sometimes changing bodies can emit unpleasant odors. Some boy students may grow hair on their faces, legs, or under their arms. Girl students may begin to grow hair on their legs and under their arms. Some of these areas may need a shave every now and then. There are many things school students need to remember to do to maintain proper hygiene.

If students do not dress neatly or smell good, other people may not want to get close to them. If students do not take care of their bodies and teeth, they may get sick.

Most students take a bath or shower each day, brush their hair and teeth several times each day, and use deodorant. Some girls shave their legs and some boys shave their faces when hair starts to grow. Shaving is not something students do until their parents show them how. Students and their parents decide when it is time to begin shaving.

When students begin to take care of their own hygiene, they may find it helpful to write down a routine or schedule to follow every day to remember to do these things. After a little practice with a daily hygiene schedule, most students have their list memorized. Some things on a hygiene schedule are done daily, some are done less often.

I can develop a personal hygiene schedule. I will try to remember to wash myself, brush my teeth, put on deodorant, and practice good hygiene habits each day. I will talk with my parents if I think I am ready to start shaving. When I use good hygiene I will not smell bad or look messy. People will want to be around me. I will try to use my schedule each day to stay clean, neat, and healthy.

Daily Hygiene – Activity Sheet

Materials

- ❑ "Daily Hygiene" experiential story for each student
- ❑ My Daily Hygiene Schedule poster.
- ❑ Hygiene Phrases and Non-Hygiene Phrases cards.
- ❑ Sticky poster tack.

Procedure

- ❑ Read "Daily Hygiene" experiential story.
- ❑ Display My Daily Hygiene Schedule poster.
- ❑ Lay Hygiene Phrases and Non-Hygiene Phrases cards on the table right side up.
- ❑ Ask students to determine which hygiene activities they might do in the morning and at night.
- ❑ Ask one student at a time to place Hygiene Phrases cards on poster with sticky poster tack.
- ❑ Discuss why Non-Hygiene Phrases cards would not be appropriate for placement on a personal hygiene schedule.
- ❑ Discuss the benefit of developing a personal hygiene schedule.
- ❑ Discuss where a personal hygiene schedule could be posted in a student's home and why.

My Daily Hygiene Schedule Poster

Directions: Enlarge and paste on poster board for poster. Copy for handout.

QUEST Program II: Social Skills Curriculum for Middle School Students with Autism
© by JoEllen Cumpata and Susan Fell. Future Horizons, Inc.

My Daily Hygiene Schedule

In the morning I will …

❑ _____

❑ _____

❑ _____

❑ _____

❑ _____

At night I will …

❑ _____

❑ _____

❑ _____

❑ _____

❑ _____

Once a week I will …

❑ _____

Once a month I will …

❑ _____

Hygiene Phrases and Non-Hygiene Phrases Cards

Directions: Enlarge and copy on colored paper, laminate, and cut into cards for poster. Copy directly for handout.

Hygiene Phrases

Wash my body in the shower with soap and water

Brush my teeth

Wash my body in the bathtub with soap and water

Wash my hands with soap and water

Put my dirty clothes in the _____

Put on deodorant

Put on clean clothes

Shave my face

Shave my legs/underarms

Brush my hair

Comb my hair

Trim my nails

Get my hair cut

QUEST Program II: Social Skills Curriculum for Middle School Students with Autism
© by JoEllen Cumpata and Susan Fell. Future Horizons, Inc.

Non-Hygiene Related Phrases

Walk the dog
Watch TV
Feed the fish
Listen to music
Gather my school supplies
Count my money
Fly a kite
Take a nap
Kiss my parents good-bye
Read a book
Take a walk
Do a dance
Lie on my bed
Water the plants
Go to a movie
Call a friend
Run around the block
Sing a song

Daily Hygiene – Activity Sheet

Materials

- ❑ "Daily Hygiene" experiential story for each student
- ❑ My Daily Hygiene Schedule handout
- ❑ Hygiene Phrases handout
- ❑ Pencils
- ❑ Magazines
- ❑ Scissors
- ❑ Glue Sticks

Procedure

- ❑ Read "Daily Hygiene" experiential story.
- ❑ Give each student a Daily Hygiene Schedule and Hygiene Phrases handout.
- ❑ Let students create their own schedule using magazines, drawings or writings to illustrate.
- ❑ Share schedules with the group.
- ❑ Laminate Schedules and ask students to use at home.
- ❑ Discuss proper location for home use.

QUEST Program II: Social Skills Curriculum for Middle School Students with Autism
© by JoEllen Cumpata and Susan Fell. Future Horizons, Inc.

QUEST Program II UPDATE!

Dear Parent,

This week your child has been working hard in QUEST Program II to master the skill of

Personal Hygiene

Together we have learned:

- Ways students are beginning to care for themselves.

- Why it is important to maintain proper hygiene.

- How to use a daily hygiene schedule at home.

You can reinforce the learning at home by:

- Asking your child what good hygiene is.

- Reminding your child why we practice good hygiene.
  e.g., "Don't forget your deodorant so you smell good. You look very neat today with your hair brushed that way."

- Reading over your child's daily hygiene schedule and deciding where it should be placed in your home — suggested location is child's bedroom or bathroom.

Important note – many of our students stated that they prefer having their parent remind them of hygiene. Our goal is to develop independence in our students. Maintaining personal hygiene is a great way to begin this journey.

Thanks for your help!

Asking for Help – Experiential Story

In school, teachers and classroom assistants are responsible for helping students understand a lot of information. This is their job. Most adults in a school want to be helpful.

Students in school learn many things. In order to learn, students must do assignments in class, work in groups with other students, and complete homework. Sometimes students become confused, don't hear a direction or need someone to explain how to do something. All students have questions sometimes. When students need help in class, it is important that they ask for it.

When students have a question about the lesson or need help they should

- Wait until the teacher is done talking.

- Raise their hand.

- When the teacher or classroom assistant calls their name or comes to help, the student should explain the problem.

- Say, "Thank you," after the teacher or classroom assistant has been helpful.

Sometimes students have a thought, a question, or a concern that is not related to the topic a teacher is discussing. Teachers are interested in students' thoughts, but usually they want to help students understand the topic they are discussing during class. When students ask unrelated questions, teachers may become annoyed. Students should wait until class is over to talk with their teachers about thoughts that are not related to the topic or class lesson. Usually teachers are happy to talk about interesting ideas or answer questions that aren't related to the lesson after class.

In certain emergency situations, students should always interrupt a teacher to ask for help. These include nose bleeds, vomiting, or times when a student may be sick or in danger.

When students ask for help, they can get their work done. Completing work is one way students can be successful in school. When students wait until class is over to discuss interesting thoughts or questions that are not related to the topic or class lesson, teachers will have time to talk and not feel annoyed. I will try to ask for help when I am confused or need someone to explain how to do something. I will try to wait until class is done to talk with my teacher about things that are not related to the lesson. Asking for help in class is a way I can be a successful school student.

QUEST Program II: Social Skills Curriculum for Middle School Students with Autism
© by JoEllen Cumpata and Susan Fell. Future Horizons, Inc.

Asking for Help – Activity Sheet

Materials

- ❑ "Asking for Help" experiential story for each student
- ❑ Asking for Help handout for each student
- ❑ Asking for Help scenario cards for each student

Procedure

- ❑ Read "Asking for Help" experiential story.
- ❑ Give Asking for Help handout to each student.
- ❑ Give a set of Asking for Help scenario cards to each student.
- ❑ Ask student to read the first card and consider if they would ask for help if they were in the situation on the card, and to hold up either their Ask for Help or Don't Ask for Help cards.
- ❑ Ask students to place cards in the correct position on their Asking for Help handout.
- ❑ Discuss correct and incorrect responses.

Asking for Help handout and scenario cards

Sometimes in middle school, students need to ask for help. Read through the cards and decide when you would ask for help. Put the card in the correct box.

Directions: Copy on colored paper, laminate, and cut into cards.

Ask for Help

Don't Ask for Help

You did not hear what your teacher assigned for homework.

Another student asks you a question while the teacher is talking.

You think the assignment is stupid.

You don't understand the first question on your test.

You feel tired and don't want to take your test.

You do not have a pencil.

You have work to do but would rather play on the computer.

You left your book in your locker.

The test is
too long.

You don't
understand how
to begin your
science lab.

You left your lunch
at home.

You cannot get
your locker open.

You don't like to
get sweaty in P.E.

You don't like to
swim during P.E.

You sneeze and
get it on your
hands.

You feel sick.

QUEST Program II: Social Skills Curriculum for Middle School Students with Autism
© by JoEllen Cumpata and Susan Fell. Future Horizons, Inc.

Another student tells you that you don't need to turn in your homework.

Another student is not prepared and asks you to give them your homework.

You cannot find your homework.

You did not do your homework.

You don't have enough time to finish your test.

The teacher is talking too loud.

You are hungry and it is not lunchtime for another two hours.

You need to go to the bathroom.

QUEST Program II UPDATE!

Dear Parent,
This week your child has been working hard in QUEST Program II to master the skill of

Asking for Help

Together we have learned:

- When it is appropriate to ask for help.

- Why it is important to get help from others when you need it.

- What emergency situations may require interrupting an adult, i.e., bloody nose, feeling like you will vomit, etc.

- How to ask for help in a classroom:

  1. Wait until the teacher is done talking.

  2. Raise your hand.

  3. Explain your problem when the teacher comes over to you.

  4. Say, "Thank you," for the help.

You can reinforce the learning at home by:

- Encouraging your child to try to accomplish things for themselves when they are able. For example, you might say, "I know it can be frustrating when you can't do it on the first try, but see if you can try again. I know you can do it!"

- Reminding your child to wait until you are done talking to ask for your help, e.g., "I need for you to wait until I am done talking before you ask me a question. Next time I will not answer you unless you wait until I am done talking."

Thanks for your help!

QUEST Program II: Social Skills Curriculum for Middle School Students with Autism
© by JoEllen Cumpata and Susan Fell. Future Horizons, Inc.

Creating a Workspace and Completing Work – Experiential Story

In school, students are expected to complete work. Students work in class and at home. They read, listen, write assignments, study, and sometimes work with other students in a group.

Sometimes students like the schoolwork and homework they are given. Sometimes they don't. Sometimes students think the work is interesting and fun. Sometimes students think the work is boring and silly. All schoolwork needs to be completed and turned in, even if students think the work is boring and silly. Completing homework and schoolwork helps students learn more and get good grades.

Teachers need to get completed school and homework back from students so they will know the student has learned something, and so they can give the student a grade. This is part of each teacher's job.

Creating a workspace at school and at home is one way that students can make completing work a bit easier, and get schoolwork done quickly. A workspace should be free from clutter, have good lighting and school supplies within easy reach. When students have all the supplies they need, good lighting and a regular work routine, it is easier to complete work, get good grades, and be a successful student.

Sometimes school students try to do their work in front of a TV, while they are talking on the telephone, playing a computer game, or eating food. These things may be enjoyable, but usually students take a lot more time to complete work when they are distracted. It is best for students to keep these kinds of distractions out of their workspace.

Sometimes when students have a lot of work to do, or if the work is very hard, it is helpful to do a little bit at a time. Many students work at home or school for 20 - 30 minutes at a time, and then take a short break (about 10 minutes). During break time, students can get a drink or snack, stretch or use the bathroom before they do more work.

I can set up a workspace at home and at school so I have all my supplies handy and get my schoolwork done quickly. When I have a clean, organized workspace I will not be distracted when I work. I will try to complete all my schoolwork and homework, even when I think it is boring or silly. When my work is too hard, I can take short rest breaks at home or in school, and then get back to work. When I complete my work, my teacher will know I have learned something and I will get a good grade. This is one way I can be a successful school student.

Creating a Workspace and Completing Work – Activity Sheet

Materials

- ❑ "Creating a Workspace and Completing Work" experiential story.
- ❑ Design Your Workspace poster
- ❑ Workspace Items
- ❑ Sticky poster tack

Procedure

- ❑ Read the "Creating a Workspace and Completing Work" experiential story.
- ❑ Display Design Your Workspace poster in the classroom.
- ❑ Spread Workspace Items on the table.
- ❑ Ask students to select one item, determine if it would be appropriate for a workspace, and if so, place it on the poster with sticky poster tack.
- ❑ Discuss selections.
- ❑ Allow students to rearrange board as they have their turn.

Design Your Workspace poster

Directions: Enlarge and paste on poster board, laminate.
Copy on 11 x 7 paper for handout.

Workspace Items

Directions: Enlarge and copy on colored paper, cut out.
Copy for handout.

My Workspace

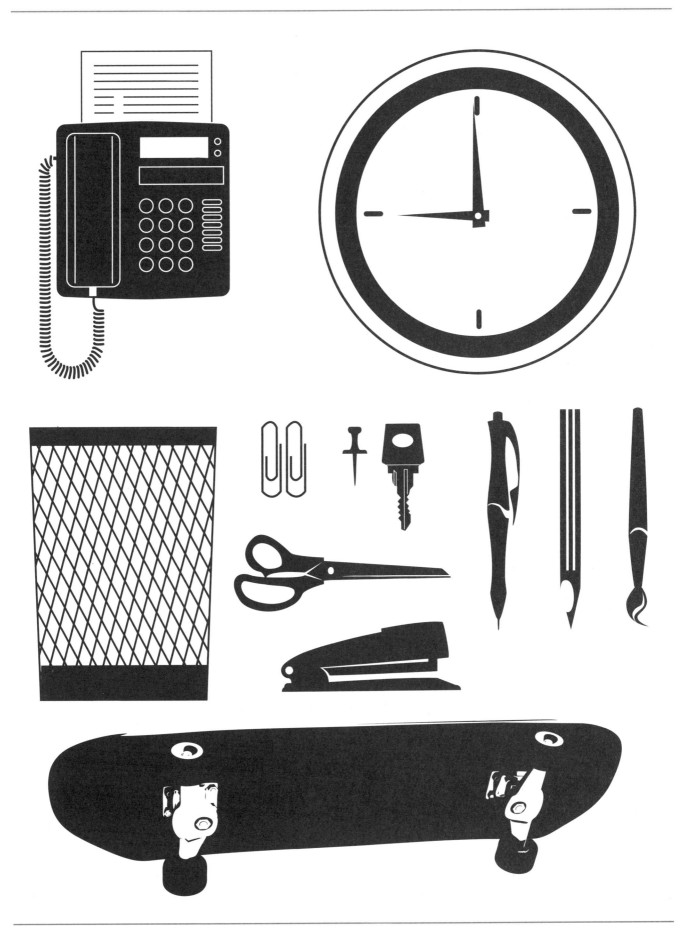

Creating a Workspace and Completing Work – Activity Sheet

Materials

- ❑ "Creating a Workspace and Completing Work" experiential story
- ❑ Designing Your Workspace handout for each student
- ❑ Workspace Items handouts for each student
- ❑ Scissors
- ❑ Glue sticks
- ❑ Crayons/markers (optional)

Procedure

- ❑ Read the Creating a "Work Space and Completing Work" experiential story.
- ❑ Remind students of Designing Your Workspace poster activity.
- ❑ Pass out Workspace Items handout, scissors and glue sticks for each student.
- ❑ Ask students to select items they feel they would need in their workspace, cut them out and glue to design their own space.
- ❑ Share with the group.

QUEST Program II UPDATE!

Dear Parent,

This week your child has been working hard in QUEST Program II to master the skill of

Creating a Workspace and Completing Work

Together we have learned:

- Why it is important to complete school and homework, even when it seems boring or silly

- How to choose appropriate items for a workspace, and recognize distractions

- The importance of establishing a nightly homework routine

You can reinforce the learning at home by:

- Reminding your child why completing work (even seemingly boring or silly work) is important. For example, you might say, "I know this seems boring to you, but your teacher needs this assignment in order to give you a grade."

- Complimenting your child when they complete difficult work. A comment such as "You have been working so hard! I know you don't enjoy doing your math. How about a five-minute milk and cookie break and then back to work? I will set the timer" is appropriate.

- Helping your child design a homework space, including:

  1. Appropriate lighting

  2. Minimal distractions (no TV, computer games, phone inaccessible)

  3. Extra school supplies (paper, pencils, calculator)

- Maintaining a nightly homework routine. You might say, "It's 5:45. Fifteen minutes more of your computer game and then it is homework time."

Thanks for your help!

QUEST Program II: Social Skills Curriculum for Middle School Students with Autism
© by JoEllen Cumpata and Susan Fell. Future Horizons, Inc.

Organizing Work and Using an Assignment Book – Experiential Story

Students go to several classes, have many books, and different teachers. Teachers in school assign class work, group projects, homework, and daily assignments. When students turn in assignments on time, they get better grades and feel comfortable and confident in class.

Sometimes students can't find their pencil or book when class begins. Sometimes students forget assignments or lose work that has been completed. When students aren't prepared and don't turn in assignments they will get a lower grade. Teachers may also be annoyed when students aren't prepared.

One way school students keep track of supplies and assignments is by keeping an organized binder, backpack, and locker. Students keep everything they need each day in their backpack and locker. Some items that students need every day are:

- Pencils

- Notebook paper

- Assignment notebook

- Completed work

- Books

Students need to remember a lot of information if they want to get their schoolwork and homework done. Most students use an assignment book to help them stay organized. The book is like a calendar. There is a space to write down assignments for each class. Students bring their assignment book and a pencil to each class, and then home at night, so they will know what they need to do for homework.

Keeping track of assignments and supplies can help students to be prepared. When students are prepared, they feel more comfortable and confident in class. I can organize my binder and backpack so that I am prepared, and have all the supplies I need in class. When I am prepared I will feel more comfortable and confident. I will be able to find my assignments and supplies and turn work in on time. My teachers will be able to give me a good grade for my work. This is a way I can be a successful student.

Organizing Work and Using an Assignment Book – Activity Sheet

Materials

- ❑ "Organizing Work and Using an Assignment Book" experiential story for each student
- ❑ Assignment Book poster (Use page from current assignment book or enlarge samples enclosed)
- ❑ Sample Assignment cards
- ❑ Wet-erase markers
- ❑ Tissue or wet wipes

Procedure

- ❑ Read the "Organizing Work and Using an Assignment Book" experiential story.
- ❑ Display the Assignment Book poster in the classroom.
- ❑ Explain to students that they will be selecting make-believe assignments and writing them in the correct location on the poster.
- ❑ Lay Sample Assignment cards face-down in the middle of the table.
- ❑ Select student to choose card and write assignment on the poster.
- ❑ Talk about possible abbreviations student could use.

Alternate Activity

Complete individual assignment books. Copy assignment book pages for each student. Choose one Sample Assignment card at a time and ask group to put assignment in proper place on their handout. Share with group.

Sample Assignment cards

Directions: Copy on colored paper, laminate, and cut into cards.

QUEST Program II: Social Skills Curriculum for Middle School Students with Autism
© by JoEllen Cumpata and Susan Fell. Future Horizons, Inc.

Math
pages 27-28
Odd problems only

Science
Evaporation lab
due Tuesday

English
Study for spelling
test Friday

Social Studies
Current events

Math
Chapter 2 Quiz

Science
Chapter 4-5 test
Thursday

English
Poem

Social Studies
Choose topic for
report

Math
Workbook pages
34-37

Science
Density lab
questions 1-12

English
Choose book for
report

Social Studies
Folders due

Health
Project outline

Foods
Create lunch menu

French
Vocabulary sheet

Reading
Read Sweet Dried
Apples story

QUEST Program II: Social Skills Curriculum for Middle School Students with Autism
© by JoEllen Cumpata and Susan Fell. Future Horizons, Inc.

Reading
Book report due

English
Put vocabulary words into sentences

Math
Remember to bring calculator

Social Studies
Color states map

Art
Finish string project

Music
Get parent signature on field trip permission slip

P.E.
Bring uniform

Math
Complete worksheet numbers 1-17 odd only

Organizing Work and Using an Assignment Book – Activity Sheet

Materials

- ❑ "Organizing Work and Using an Assignment Book" experiential story
- ❑ Sample binder with color-coded folder for each class, pencil case, two pencils (for each student)
- ❑ Copy of student class schedules
- ❑ Markers

It is important to discuss this activity with each student's general education teacher, special education teacher, or case coordinator prior to restructuring their binder.

Procedure

- ❑ Read the "Organizing Work and Using an Assignment Book" experiential story.
- ❑ Show sample binder to students and explain how color-coded sections can help them organize their day.
- ❑ Assist each student in organizing their current binder according to their daily schedule. Make sure to include a folder for homework and for information to share with parent.

QUEST Program II: Social Skills Curriculum for Middle School Students with Autism
© by JoEllen Cumpata and Susan Fell. Future Horizons, Inc.

QUEST Program II UPDATE!

Dear Parent,

This week your child has been working hard in QUEST Program II to master the skill of

Organizing Work and Using an Assignment Book

Together we have learned and practiced:

- Finding the appropriate space to write in an assignment book

- Accurately writing assignments and using abbreviations when possible

- Ways to organize student binders to easily locate classwork and homework

You can reinforce the learning at home by:

- Asking to see your child's assignment book each night

- Helping your child keep their binder organized by

   1. Looking through it with your child once weekly

   2. Throwing out unneeded material

   3. Sorting assignments into proper folders

   4. Restocking pencils, paper, etc.

- Reminding your child to pack their binder with needed supplies nightly

Thanks for your help!

Successful Student Bingo – Unit Summary

Materials

❑ Being a Successful Student Takes Skills handout for each student

❑ Pencils

❑ Successful Student Bingo card for each student

❑ Blank sheets of paper (approximately 3" x 3")

❑ Bingo Markers (run off on colored paper, laminate, and cut into small squares)

❑ Small storage container

Procedure

❑ Review skills discussed in Unit 1 - Greetings, Paying Attention, Daily Hygiene, Asking for Help, Creating a Homework Space and Getting Organized.

❑ Call on students to complete Being a Successful Student Takes Skills handout together.

❑ Ask students to copy items from Being a Successful Student Takes Skills handout to spaces on their Successful Student Bingo cards (make sure students put only one item in each space and write items in random order on Bingo sheet).

❑ Write items on small slips of paper, fold and put in storage container.

❑ Pull one item out at a time and have students cover that item on their bingo sheet with a Bingo Marker.

❑ First student to fill a straight line is the winner.

Alternate Activity

To save time, students can write items directly on Bingo sheet without using Being a Successful Student Takes Skills handout. Items must still be written on small slips of paper to be used during game.

QUEST Program II: Social Skills Curriculum for Middle School Students with Autism
© by JoEllen Cumpata and Susan Fell. Future Horizons, Inc.

Being a Successful Student Takes Skills!

1. Greetings

_____

_____

_____

_____

2. Paying Attention

_____

_____

_____

_____

3. Daily Hygiene

_____

_____

_____

_____

4. Asking for Help

_____

_____

_____

_____

_____

5. Creating a Workspace and Completing Work

_____

_____

_____

_____

_____

6. Organizing Work and Using an Assignment Book

_____

_____

_____

_____

_____

QUEST Program II: Social Skills Curriculum for Middle School Students with Autism
© by JoEllen Cumpata and Susan Fell. Future Horizons, Inc.

Successful Student Bingo

Directions: Copy on colored paper, laminate, and cut into cards.

		QUEST		

Bingo Markers

Directions: Copy several sheets on colored paper,
laminate, and cut into squares.

QUEST Program II Unit One
School Survival Basics Unit Evaluation

Student Name _____ Date _____

Evaluator _____

We have just completed a unit in QUEST Program II on School Survival Basics. Please complete the rating scale below to assist us in determining how well the student above has generalized the skills taught, and if you have noticed improvement in their level of skill over the past six weeks. Check all boxes that apply below.

O=Often S=Sometimes N=Never I=Improvement   **How Often Skill Is Observed**

Skill	O	S	N	I
Greeting others Stand an arm's length away, smile, use good eye contact, say, "Hello," hug family, shake hands with "important" people, wave when someone is far away or in quiet places.				
Paying attention when others talk Use good eye contact, keep back straight, hands and feet still, quiet until the other person is finished.				
Practicing good hygiene Independently use a hygiene schedule to bathe, dress appropriately, groom self, and put dirty clothes in hamper.				
Asking for help Wait until the adult is done talking, let them know you need assistance, and say thank you.				
Creating a work space and completing work Design and use a work space with all necessary supplies, good lighting, and minimal distractions. Break work up into segments. Use appropriate rest breaks during work time.				
Organizing work and using an assignment book Use a folder system within each binder to organize work. Independently use an assignment book to keep track of assignments. Pack backpack nightly with needed materials.				

Comments _____

Thank you for your input!

Unit 2

Understanding and Managing Emotions

Goal

To develop and improve emotional identification and management skills

Objectives

➤ To distinguish the facial expressions, tone, and body language associated with different types of emotion, and recognize that all people experience emotion.

➤ To identify uncomfortable feelings (anger, sadness, frustration, embarrassment) and understand the importance of relaxing and talking to an adult when students experience uncomfortable feelings.

➤ To learn and practice acceptable anger management strategies.

➤ To better understand the experience and consequences of stress and learn stress management techniques.

➤ To learn and understand the importance of negotiating differences with others.

➤ To demonstrate knowledge of effective problem-solving steps.

QUEST Program II: Social Skills Curriculum for Middle School Students with Autism

Experiential Stories, Activities, and Parent Updates

Stories can be read by parents, teachers or students. Often students gain a deeper understanding of skills when stories can be discussed in detail in a group setting. Asking students to summarize paragraphs, relate their personal experiences and complete activities are all effective ways to increase generalization of skills. Parent Updates provide additional ways to continue learning at home. The letter "A" denotes advanced sections appropriate for students in their second or third year of the program.

Topics included in this unit are:

1. Understanding Feelings

2. Uncomfortable Feelings

3. Getting Angry and Calming Down

4. Stress Management

5. Negotiating With Others - A

6. Problem Solving – A

Understanding Feelings – Experiential Story

It is normal for students to experience many different types of feelings every day. Happiness, excitement, anger, and frustration are all examples of the types of feelings students may experience at school or home.

Having many different feelings is a normal part of being a person. Some feelings, such as happiness or excitement, make us feel good. When people are happy they stand up tall, smile, and sometimes even laugh. When students are excited they may move around a lot, talk faster or with a louder voice, or even touch or hug other students.

Some feelings, such as anger, sadness, or frustration may make our bodies feel uncomfortable. When students are angry, sad, or frustrated they often frown, cross their arms, cry, or even yell. Sometimes students who are very angry make a fist, pound a desk, or throw things.

When students are interested they sit up straight, keep their hands and feet still, and make eye contact with the person who is talking. When students are bored they slouch, lie on their desk, and look away from the person who is talking.

Standing up tall, smiling, giving good eye contact, folding our arms, and making a fist are all ways we can use our bodies to let other people know how we are feeling. This type of communication is called "body language."

Sometimes we can tell how someone else is feeling by looking at their body language. We can tell if a person is interested or bored, happy or sad, excited, frustrated, or angry by looking at their body language.

All people have many different feelings. I have different feelings too. I can use body language to let people know how I feel. People can tell how I am feeling by looking at my body language. I can try to understand how my family, friends, and teachers are feeling by looking at their body language.

Understanding Feelings – Activity Sheet

Materials

- ❑ "Understanding Feelings" experiential story
- ❑ Understanding Feelings handout
- ❑ Scissors
- ❑ Glue sticks
- ❑ Magazines
- ❑ Crayons or markers

Procedure

- ❑ Read "Understanding Feelings" experiential story.
- ❑ Pass out an Understanding Feelings handout to each student.
- ❑ Have students draw or cut and glue pictures from magazines to illustrate emotions discussed in experiential story.
- ❑ Discuss

Understanding Feelings

All people have emotions. Sometimes people show their feelings by using their bodies. This is called body language. These are examples of people feeling emotions and using body language.

Happy	Sad

Angry	Excited

Interested	Bored

QUEST Program II: Social Skills Curriculum for Middle School Students with Autism
© by JoEllen Cumpata and Susan Fell. Future Horizons, Inc.

Understanding Feelings – Activity Sheet

Materials

- ❑ "Understanding Feelings" experiential story
- ❑ Feelings flash cards

Procedure

- ❑ Read "Understanding Feelings" experiential story.
- ❑ Introduce Feelings flash cards. Give one card to each student to read and demonstrate.
- ❑ Mix cards upside-down on table.
- ❑ Have one student choose a card and act it out for the group.
- ❑ The first student to correctly identify the feeling chooses the next card.

Feelings flash cards

Directions: Copy on colored paper, laminate, and cut into cards.

Happy

Sad

Angry

Excited

Interested

Bored

QUEST Program II: Social Skills Curriculum for Middle School Students with Autism
© by JoEllen Cumpata and Susan Fell. Future Horizons, Inc.

Understanding Feelings – Activity Sheet

Materials

- ❑ "Understanding Feelings" experiential story
- ❑ Understanding Feelings poster
- ❑ Feelings flash cards
- ❑ Sticky poster tack

Procedure

- ❑ Read "Understanding Feelings" experiential story.
- ❑ Indicate feelings on Understanding Feelings poster and ask students to imitate feeling.
- ❑ Place Feelings flash cards on a table.
- ❑ Ask students to choose a card, place on poster in appropriate spot using poster tack.
- ❑ Ask students to share with group a time when they felt that way.

Understanding Feelings Poster

Directions: Enlarge on copier, and paste on poster board.

Happy	Sad

Angry	Excited

Interested	Bored

Understanding Feelings – Activity Sheet

Materials

- ❑ "Understanding Feelings" experiential story
- ❑ Feelings flash cards
- ❑ Feelings scenario cards

Procedure

- ❑ Read "Understanding Feelings" experiential story.
- ❑ Review Feelings flash cards. Ask students to demonstrate each.
- ❑ Lay Feelings scenario cards upside-down on table.
- ❑ Ask student to select card, read out loud, and say or demonstrate how they would be feeling.
- ❑ Discuss responses.

Feelings scenario cards

Directions: Copy on colored paper, color code each emotion if desired, laminate, and cut into cards.

Sad

You just found out that your grandmother needs to go to the hospital.

Your best friend is home sick.

You are reading a book and the main character is made fun of by another student.

Your neighbor's dog is hit by a car.

You are watching a movie and a character in the movie learns he has cancer.

Your father tells you that he found out today that his boss is very sick.

Your best friend tells you his parents are getting a divorce.

You go to a family funeral.

QUEST Program II: Social Skills Curriculum for Middle School Students with Autism
© by JoEllen Cumpata and Susan Fell. Future Horizons, Inc.

Happy

You just found out that your grandfather won a new car.

Your best friend invites you to a party.

You are reading a book and the main character gets an A+ on his report card.

Your neighbor's dog has puppies.

You are watching a movie and a character in the movie hits a home run.

Your father tells you that he found out today that he is getting a raise in pay.

Your best friend tells you his parents said he can take a friend camping with him.

You go to a family picnic.

Excited

You just found out that your grandmother is taking you to a movie.

Your best friend just got a new computer game you really want to try.

You are reading a book and the main character has almost won a race.

Your neighbor says he will pay you to walk his dog.

You are watching a movie you really love and your mother tells you she will buy you a copy of the movie.

Your father tells you that he has a surprise for you.

Your best friend tells you his mom is pregnant.

Your parents tell you they just bought tickets to Cedar Point.

QUEST Program II: Social Skills Curriculum for Middle School Students with Autism
© by JoEllen Cumpata and Susan Fell. Future Horizons, Inc.

Angry

A student tells you that she thinks your report was stupid.

Your best friend tells you a lie.

You are reading a book and the last page is missing.

Your neighbor's dog bites you.

You are watching a movie and your mother tells you that you need to leave for the dentist.

Your friend tells you she doesn't want you to eat lunch with her anymore.

A student takes your pencil without asking.

A student pushes you down in the hall.

Bored

The teacher is talking about a book you already read.

Another student is giving a report that you are not interested in.

You can't think of anything fun to do.

You need to wait for your mother while she tries on clothes at the store.

You are watching a movie that your sister picked and you think it is uninteresting.

Your father likes to tell you all about the stock market but you are not interested.

Your best friend tells you every detail about his vacation but you really don't care.

You go to see a play that only your mother loves.

QUEST Program II: Social Skills Curriculum for Middle School Students with Autism
© by JoEllen Cumpata and Susan Fell. Future Horizons, Inc.

Interested

Your science teacher is demonstrating a lab that you have been wondering about.

You are watching a fascinating TV program.

You are reading a book about your favorite topic.

Your neighbor asks you to come over to see a remarkable trick his dog can do.

You are watching a movie you have been waiting to see for a week.

Your father tells you that he has a problem he knows you will want to hear about.

Your best friend tells you he figured out how to solve a puzzle you both have been working on.

Your best friend is presenting a surprising report to the class.

QUEST Program II UPDATE!

Dear Parent,

This week your child has been working hard in QUEST Program II to master the skill of

Understanding Feelings

Together we have learned and practiced:

- Recognizing the different body language people sometimes use when they are happy, sad, angry, excited, bored or interested.

- Appropriately identifying emotions demonstrated by peers and teachers.

- Demonstrating the body language associated with different emotions for fellow students to identify.

You can help your child practice at home by:

- Describing how you or your child are feeling.

- Identifying the body language associated with the feeling, e.g., "I can tell you are really happy because I see a big smile on your face." or "It looks like you are really angry because you just stamped your foot!" or "I bet you can tell I'm worried because I am pacing around the room."

- Call your child's attention to the body language of peers, family members, and/or characters on TV programs or in movies, e.g., "Did you see how that man crossed his arms and frowned when he talked to his son? How do you think he was feeling?" or "Wow, did you see how Uncle Jack was jumping around and talking fast and loud? It looked like he was really excited about his new boat!"

Thanks for your help!

QUEST Program II: Social Skills Curriculum for Middle School Students with Autism
© by JoEllen Cumpata and Susan Fell. Future Horizons, Inc.

Uncomfortable Feelings – Experiential Story

All students feel angry, sad, frustrated, and embarrassed sometimes. Students may feel angry or frustrated when they want something they cannot have, when others ask them to do things they don't want to do, or when they disagree with someone. Students might feel sad or embarrassed when other students don't include them in their conversation or group. Students may feel worried when they are not ready for a class project, test, or presentation.

When students experience many uncomfortable feelings in a short period of time, they may find it difficult to concentrate, do school work, or have fun doing activities they enjoy. When students let their uncomfortable feelings grow, they might yell at or hit others, throw or break things, or run and hide.

In school, yelling, throwing things, hitting, running away and hiding are against the rules. These behaviors can be dangerous to students. It is important for students to try to relax when they feel uncomfortable.

When students feel uncomfortable feelings, they usually notice changes in the way their body and head feels. Students may feel like they want to leave the room, their head or stomach may begin to hurt, they may feel hot, they may feel like they want to cry, or they may start saying loud angry things to other students or adults.

Some students have relaxing things they do whenever they start to feel uncomfortable. Restful, relaxing activities help students calm down and stay in class. Students relax in different ways. Some ways students relax are:

- Counting to ten

- Watching a sand timer

- Closing their eyes

- Putting cool water on their face or wrist

- Going to a quiet place in the classroom and taking a time-out

- Enhaling slowly through their nose, and then exhaling through their mouth

- Saying relaxing things in their head

- Writing down feelings

- Using Koosh balls, playdough, or other relaxation toys

Sometimes students find it helpful to talk to someone when they have uncomfortable feelings. Students may not know why they are feeling uncomfortable but it can be helpful to talk about it anyway. Students and adults can talk about feelings and decide what to do about them. This usually makes students feel better.

I know I may have many different feelings each day. Sometimes I may have uncomfortable feelings. Everyone has uncomfortable feelings sometimes. I will try to relax when I have uncomfortable feelings. I will try to talk with an adult when I feel angry, sad, afraid, or have other uncomfortable feelings. Relaxing and talking with an adult will make me feel better.

QUEST Program II: Social Skills Curriculum for Middle School Students with Autism
© by JoEllen Cumpata and Susan Fell. Future Horizons, Inc.

Uncomfortable Feelings – Activity Sheet

Materials

- ❏ "Uncomfortable Feelings" experiential story
- ❏ Sometimes We Feel Uncomfortable poster and handout
- ❏ Body Feelings cards
- ❏ De-escalation cards
- ❏ Sticky poster tack

Procedure

- ❏ Read "Uncomfortable Feelings" experiential story.
- ❏ Ask students to look through Body Feelings cards and, one-by-one, place cards on the Sometimes We Feel Uncomfortable poster with poster tack to indicate what they experience when they have uncomfortable feelings.
- ❏ Have students identify one or two things that trigger uncomfortable feelings for them.
- ❏ Ask students to look through De-escalation cards and choose one that they would try when feeling uncomfortable. Place on bottom of poster with poster tack.
- ❏ Ask students to complete their Sometimes We Feel Uncomfortable handout.
- ❏ Share with the group.

Sometimes We Feel Uncomfortable poster

Directions: Copy for student handouts. Enlarge to poster size, attach to poster board, and laminate.

Sometimes We Feel Uncomfortable

This is how my body feels when I'm uncomfortable.

To relax, I like to

_____

QUEST Program II: Social Skills Curriculum for Middle School Students with Autism
© by JoEllen Cumpata and Susan Fell. Future Horizons, Inc.

Body Feelings cards

Directions: Copy on colored paper, laminate, cut into strips.

Sweaty Palms	Hot
Upset Stomach	Sore Head
Heart Beating Fast	Tired
Want to Run	Want to Cry
Want to Hit	Want to Throw Up
Yell at People	Stop Working

De-escalation cards

Directions: Copy on colored paper, laminate, cut into strips.

Read a Book	Count to Ten
Watch a Timer	Write Down My Feelings
Close My Eyes	Put Water On My Face
Breathe Slowly	Put On Hand Lotion
Think Good Thoughts	Drink Water
Rub Something in My Hands	Take a Walk
Listen to Music	Talk with Someone

QUEST Program II UPDATE!

Dear Parent,

This week your child has been working hard in QUEST Program II to master the skill of

Recognizing and Managing Uncomfortable Feelings

Together we have learned and practiced:

- Ways to recognize uncomfortable feelings including anger, sadness, frustration, anxiety, and embarrassment.

- Appropriate relaxation techniques.

- The importance of talking about uncomfortable feelings with an adult.

You can help your child practice at home by:

- Practicing relaxation techniques with your child during calm times, and reminding them to use their technique when they are upset.

Deep breathing	Listening to music	Counting to ten
Taking a walk	Writing in a journal	Drawing
Closing eyes	Putting cool water on face or wrists	
Taking a time-out	Squeezing sensory object	

- Modeling relaxation techniques when your child is near, e.g., "I had such a stressful day, I think I am going to take a long bubble bath and listen to music" or "I'm feeling very frustrated right now, and I need to go to my room for a while and relax before we talk about this."

- Encouraging your child to work through their upsetting feelings, e.g., "I can see you are upset, why don't you relax in your room for ten minutes and then we can talk." or "I know you are frustrated that you need to stop your computer game right now. Why don't you take a few deep breaths and grab your stress ball before we leave?"

Thanks for your help!

QUEST Program II: Social Skills Curriculum for Middle School Students with Autism
© by JoEllen Cumpata and Susan Fell. Future Horizons, Inc.

Getting Angry and Calming Down – Experiential Story

Everyone gets angry sometimes. People get angry when they want something they cannot have, when others ask them to do things they don't want to do, and when they disagree with someone. Getting angry is an uncomfortable feeling.

When students get angry they usually frown, shout, or say loud words. Some students look sad and don't say anything when they are angry. Sometimes when people are angry their stomach or head hurts, and they may feel hot. Students who are very angry may want to throw things, hit or destroy things, use inappropriate or mean language, or run and hide.

In school, yelling, throwing things, hitting, using inappropriate language, or running away and hiding are against the rules. These behaviors can be dangerous to students. It is important for students to try to calm down when they are angry so they can follow school rules, talk about what is making them angry, and start to feel better.

When students relax, they will feel calmer. They can usually talk about their anger, work out a solution to their problem, and feel better.

Four things students can do when they are feeling angry are:

1. Ignore

2. Relax

3. Talk it out

4. Get adult help

When students follow these steps they can usually calm down and solve problems before they become too angry.

I can follow the four steps when I am feeling angry. I can try to ignore the situation. If that doesn't work, I can try to relax and talk it out. Lastly, I can get adult help if I need it. I can handle my anger without breaking school rules.

Getting Angry and Calming Down – Activity Sheet

Materials

- ❑ "Getting Angry and Calming Down" experiential story
- ❑ Getting Angry scenario cards
- ❑ De-escalation Steps cards

Procedure

- ❑ Read "Getting Angry and Calming Down" experiential story.
- ❑ Pass out a set of four De-escalation Steps cards to each student (ignore, relax, talk it out, ask an adult for help).
- ❑ Describe each method.
- ❑ Ask a student to choose a Getting Angry scenario card and read aloud.
- ❑ Have group hold up De-escalation Steps card they feel would work best in this scenario.
- ❑ Ask students to role-play suggested method.
- ❑ Brainstorm additional ways students could de-escalate the situation.

QUEST Program II: Social Skills Curriculum for Middle School Students with Autism
© by JoEllen Cumpata and Susan Fell. Future Horizons, Inc.

Getting Angry scenario cards

Directions: Copy on colored paper, laminate, and cut into strips.

Peter refuses to get off the computer when you have asked him nicely.

Sean always wants to hold your hand in the halls. You have asked him to stop many times because you don't like this. Sean doesn't stop.

Jeff likes to put the binders in alphabetical order. You think this is a waste of time.

Mike wants you to be his best friend and he gets angry when he sees you talking to other students. You prefer to have a lot of friends.

The teacher asks you to answer a question. You don't like to talk in front of the class.

The teacher tells you to put your assignment away, but you have not completed it yet.

The teacher puts you in a group with Paul. Paul has made fun of you in the past.

The teacher tells you to stop talking.

Randy doesn't save a seat for you at lunch.

Emily picks her nose. You tell her to stop every time she does this, but she keeps on doing it.

Pamela takes your seat.

Robert likes to sit next to you in class. Eric sits in Robert's seat to make him mad.

The teacher never lets you finish your sentence.

The teacher only calls on you once each class.

QUEST Program II: Social Skills Curriculum for Middle School Students with Autism
© by JoEllen Cumpata and Susan Fell. Future Horizons, Inc.

It is 2nd hour. You are worried that you didn't study enough for your math test 5th hour.

Jake trips in the hall and you see several students laugh at him.

Sandy cuts in front of you in the lunch line.

The teacher asks students to turn in their homework and you remember you left it on the kitchen table at home.

Brad keeps coughing in class. You can't concentrate.

De-escalation Steps cards

Directions: Copy on colored paper, one set (ignore, relax, ask an adult for help, talk it out) per student. Laminate, and cut into cards.

Ignore

- Walk away
- Think about something else
- Say, "Ignore it," in your head

Relax

- Count to ten
- Take deep breaths
- Think about nice things
- Put cool water on your face

Ask an Adult for Help

- Find an adult you trust
- Raise your hand when in class
- Tell the adult you need help
- Explain the situation

Talk It Out

- Speak calmly
- Tell your side
- Listen to their side
- Brainstorm possible solutions
- Agree on a solution

QUEST Program II: Social Skills Curriculum for Middle School Students with Autism
© by JoEllen Cumpata and Susan Fell. Future Horizons, Inc.

QUEST Program II UPDATE!

Dear Parent,

This week your child has been working hard in QUEST Program II to master the skill of

Managing Anger and Calming Down

Together we have learned:

- All people get angry.

- It is dangerous and inappropriate to throw, yell, call names, or run and hide when you are angry.

- At school there are four ways to handle anger:

  1. Ignore

  2. Relax

  3. Talk it out

  4. Get an adult

You can help your child practice at home by:

- Modeling good anger management, e.g., "Boy what a day I had! I really feel angry. I think I will take Spot for a long walk. Want to come?" or "I feel so angry right now! I need to step outside to relax, then we need to talk about this."

- Reminding your child of positive ways to manage their own anger, e.g., "You seem very upset, why don't we both take a few deep breaths and talk about it." or "I know you are angry at your teacher right now. Why don't we practice what you can say to her next time."

Thanks for your help!

Stress Management – Experiential Story

Most students go to the same classes each day, have the same teachers, and the same friends. Usually students know what time they will eat, what time they will go to bed and get up in the morning, and what to expect the next day.

Even though most students follow a daily school schedule, they can become overwhelmed when they have too much to do, or when things change unexpectedly. Changes can be good, like getting a new dog or going to a birthday party. Changes can also be difficult, like finding out your grandparent is in the hospital, or getting a bad grade on a test. All changes, even fun ones, can make students feel overwhelmed. This is called stress. All students feel stress from time to time. Sometimes students can even feel stress several times in one day.

Stress affects students in different ways. Stress can make a student's stomach and head hurt. Students who are stressed may feel very hungry or lose their appetite. They may feel very tired or have trouble sleeping. When students are stressed they may have a hard time concentrating or staying organized. When students feel stress they might even yell, hit, or break things. Stress is usually an uncomfortable feeling, and it can keep students from doing their best.

It is important for students to learn ways to recognize and manage their daily stress. When students manage daily stress they feel better, treat others better, and can be better students.

Students can manage stress by relaxing, staying organized, exercising, eating well, and getting enough sleep. Students can also manage stress by talking with others about the things that are bothering them, and coming up with ways to make their life more comfortable.

Everyone feels stress from time to time. If I don't manage my anger and stress I might feel tired, angry, or sick. I might yell, hit, or throw things. I might also have a difficult time paying attention and doing the things I have to do in order to be a successful student.

I will try to manage stress each day by relaxing, staying organized, exercising, eating well, and getting enough sleep. I can also manage my stress better if I talk with people I trust when I feel overwhelmed. When I manage my stress, I can pay attention in class and do my best.

QUEST Program II: Social Skills Curriculum for Middle School Students with Autism
© by JoEllen Cumpata and Susan Fell. Future Horizons, Inc.

Stress Managment – Activity Sheet

Materials

- ❑ "Stress Management" experiential story
- ❑ When Stress Takes Over poster
- ❑ Stress Definition poster
- ❑ How Does Your Stress Level Measure Up quiz
- ❑ I Can Handle Stress poster
- ❑ Pencils

Procedure

- ❑ Read "Stress Management" experiential story.
- ❑ Use Stress definition and When Stress Takes Over poster to continue discussion about what stress is and how it can negatively impact students.
- ❑ Pass out How Does Your Stress Level Measure Up quiz.
- ❑ Ask students to complete quiz. Reassure them that this is not graded and is only to determine the level of stress in their lives over the past week.
- ❑ Use I Can Handle Stress poster to initiate discussion regarding stress management techniques.

When Stress Takes Over poster

Directions: Enlarge and paste on poster board.

When Stress Takes Over

IRRITABILITY!

EXHAUSTION!

POOR CONCENTRATION

STOMACHACHE!

HEADACHE!

EATING TOO MUCH OR TOO LITTLE

Stress is...

The way our body responds to life events and change.

How Does Your Stress Level Measure Up?

Read the questions below. Think about your last week in school. Circle "YES" or "NO" for each. Then read the directions on the back to see just how stressed out you are.

In the last week, did you

Take a test?	YES	NO
Have an argument?	YES	NO
Get to school or class late?	YES	NO
Meet someone new?	YES	NO
Get a long-term assignment?	YES	NO
Have a substitute teacher?	YES	NO
Fail to complete an assignment?	YES	NO
Feel embarrassed?	YES	NO
Say no to a friend?	YES	NO
Compete in anything?	YES	NO
Have too much homework?	YES	NO
Disagree with your teacher?	YES	NO
Plan an event?	YES	NO
Feel sick?	YES	NO
Lose something?	YES	NO
Forget to do an assignment?	YES	NO
Get invited somewhere?	YES	NO
Get a paper or test grade?	YES	NO
Feel left out?	YES	NO
Answer a question in class?	YES	NO

Count up the number of "YES" answers you circled. Check the chart below to see how your stress level measures up.

0 – 5 "YES" responses

Congratulations, you had a very relaxing week! Don't worry! Be happy!

6 – 10 "YES" responses

Your week was a bit stressful. Hang in there!

11 – 15 "YES" responses

You experienced a stressful week. Think about ways to relax tonight.

16 – 20 "YES" responses

Your week was extremely stressful! TAKE A BREAK! You deserve it!

I Can Handle Stress poster

Directions: Enlarge and paste on poster board.

I Can Handle Stress!

No Energy?

Get plenty of sleep each night.

Eat nutritious foods.

Stay away from drugs/alcohol.

Be active.

Too Much Homework?

Talk it over with your teacher.

Get organized.

Form a homework/ study group.

Put on some background music.

Break work up into smaller segments.

Friend/Family Troubles?

Talk to someone you trust.

Problem solve.

Say, "I'm sorry."

Forgive someone.

Feeling Blue?

Read a good book.

Take a walk.

Laugh.

Watch a video.

Exercise.

Play with your pet.

Call a friend.

QUEST Program II: Social Skills Curriculum for Middle School Students with Autism
© by JoEllen Cumpata and Susan Fell. Future Horizons, Inc.

Stress Managment – Activity Sheet

Materials

- ❑ "Stress Management" experiential story
- ❑ Stress Buster Student scenario cards
- ❑ Four 8 ½ x 11 manila envelopes
- ❑ Signs of Stress cards
- ❑ Stress Buster cards
- ❑ Stress Buster poster

Procedure

- ❑ Review "Stress Managment" experiential story.
- ❑ Divide group into four teams.
- ❑ Pass a Stress Buster Student Scenario card stapled to manila envelope to each team. Envelopes should also contain set of Signs of Stress cards and set of Stress Buster cards.
- ❑ Ask students to read and discuss their scenario card with their group members.
- ❑ Ask each group to choose the Signs of Stress cards which best describe the symptoms the student in their Student Scenario card is exhibiting.
- ❑ Place on Stress Buster poster using poster tack.
- ❑ Ask each group to choose the Stress Buster cards which best describe ways the student in their Student Scenario could make life choices to better manage stress.
- ❑ Place on Stress Buster poster using poster tack.
- ❑ Discuss with the group.
- ❑ Repeat with each Student Scenario.

Stress Buster Student scenario cards

Directions: Copy on colored paper. Staple one card on top of manila envelope. Place set of Stress Buster cards and Stress Symptoms cards in envelope.

STRESS BUSTER

Student Scenario

Are you a stress buster? Read about the student below and help him find healthy ways to manage his stress.

Brian is RESPONSIBLE!

Brian gets stressed when things change unexpectedly, when he gets behind in his schoolwork, and when he feels unorganized. Brian tries to come prepared each day and get good grades, but sometimes he forgets things and gets behind in his work.

After school Brian likes to relax, watch TV, and play video games. Brian generally starts on homework in the evening, and sometimes he works very late to finish everything. Brian often has a hard time sleeping. In the morning Brian runs all over the house looking for his things. Sometimes Brian feels sick in the morning, especially if he didn't finish his work the night before. Brian is late for school often and sometimes asks to see the nurse when he isn't really sick, but just hasn't finished his homework.

QUEST Program II: Social Skills Curriculum for Middle School Students with Autism
© by JoEllen Cumpata and Susan Fell. Future Horizons, Inc.

STRESS BUSTER
Student Scenario

Are you a stress buster? Read about the student below and help her find healthy ways to manage her stress.

Sally is FRIENDLY!

Sally gets stressed when teachers are upset with her. Sally enjoys socializing with other students, and she really wants to be popular. Sally is on the girls' basketball team, in choir, and also takes dance classes after school. On weekends, Sally spends most of her time hanging out with friends, talking on Instant Messenger, or going to parties.

Sally's grades have been dropping and her parents are fed up. Sally has even started to lie to her parents about homework so she can go out with her friends. She hasn't felt like eating lately. Last weekend, Sally tried some beer at a party and she knows she will be grounded if her parents find out. Sally is angry and frustrated, but she also feels guilty because her parents and teachers are disappointed with her.

STRESS BUSTER

Student Scenario

Are you a stress buster? Read about the student below and help him find healthy ways to manage his stress.

Nick is ENTERTAINING!

In school, Nick gets stressed when teachers give too much work! Nick thinks most lectures and assignments are boring! He usually feels overwhelmed by assignments, especially long-term projects. It is very hard for Nick to sit still for long periods in class, and he finds himself acting silly or daydreaming a lot!

Nick would like to be a better student but he really likes getting attention and the work is too hard. Sometimes he goofs around or shouts out in class. Some kids think Nick is funny, but some kids think he is a pest. Nick gets detention often because of his behavior. Sometimes he tries to do his work but he forgets things and doesn't remember what the assignment is. Large projects seem too hard, and Nick doesn't know how to get started.

QUEST Program II: Social Skills Curriculum for Middle School Students with Autism
© by JoEllen Cumpata and Susan Fell. Future Horizons, Inc.

STRESS BUSTER

Student Scenario

Are you a stress buster? Read about the student below and help her find healthy ways to manage her stress.

Anna is INDEPENDENT!

In school, Anna gets stressed when things aren't done right. Teachers sometimes expect students to work as part of a group and Anna doesn't like this. Anna likes doing things her way and often other students don't do a good job. Sometimes they don't do their part at all! Anna thinks kids want to be in her group only because she will do all the work.

Anna feels frustrated and knows the kids think she is bossy. Anna yells a lot at school and at home.   She has been spending less time with friends and usually is alone in her room on weekends. Lately she has been crying a lot.

Signs of Stress cards

Directions: Copy on colored paper, laminate, and cut into cards.

Arguments with parents	**Feeling tired**
Sleeping all the time	**Can't sleep**
Easily angry - yelling a lot	**Feeling guilty**

Feeling sad

Trouble sleeping

Poor grades

Not eating well

Lying

Isolating - less time with friends

Late

Frequent detention

Forgetful

Feeling sick

Using illegal substances

Stress Buster cards

Directions: Copy on colored paper, laminate, and cut into cards.
Use different colored paper than you used for Signs of Stress cards.

Use a planner	**Talk with a teacher**
Talk with a parent	**Talk with a counselor**
Call a friend	**Exercise**

Organize backpack at night	Start a study/ homework group
Drop one after-school activity	Go get homework help
Keep extra supplies in locker	Take time for relaxation
Ask teacher for academic help	Use a sleep routine

QUEST Program II: Social Skills Curriculum for Middle School Students with Autism
© by JoEllen Cumpata and Susan Fell. Future Horizons, Inc.

Eat healthy foods

Make a social date with friends

Spend some fun time with family

Stress Buster poster

Directions: Print column headings on colored paper,
paste on poster board to create Stress Buster poster. See sample below.

Student	Signs of Stress	Stress Busters
Sally		
Nick		
Anna		
Brian		

QUEST Program II: Social Skills Curriculum for Middle School Students with Autism
© by JoEllen Cumpata and Susan Fell. Future Horizons, Inc.

Student

Signs of Stress

Stress Busters

QUEST Program II UPDATE!

Dear Parent,

This week your child has been working hard in QUEST Program II to master the skill of

Stress Management

Together we have learned that:

- Stress is the way our body responds to changes.

- All students experience stress.

- Students experience stress differently. Some have headaches or stomachaches, some notice changes in their eating or sleeping patterns, some become disorganized, and some even feel very sad or angry.

- Students can manage stress by:

  1. Practicing relaxation techniques

  2. Exercising regularly

  3. Talking it out with someone they trust

  4. Maintaining healthy nutrition and sleep patterns

  5. Taking time for fun

  6. Making positive life changes

You can help your child practice at home by:

- Modeling good stress management, e.g., "Boy what a day I had! I really feel stressed! I think I will listen to some music in the garden for awhile." or "I had such a difficult day! I feel like I need to relax tonight. How about we order a pizza and play Scrabble?"

- Reminding your child of positive ways to manage their stress, e.g., "You seem very stressed. Why don't we relax a bit and play your video game then we can talk about it?" or "Sounds like you had a stressful day. How about if you take a walk around the block and relax a bit?"

Thanks for your help!

QUEST Program II: Social Skills Curriculum for Middle School Students with Autism
© by JoEllen Cumpata and Susan Fell. Future Horizons, Inc.

Negotiating with Others – Experiential Story

Most parents spend a lot of time teaching young children how to behave, be safe, and follow directions. Usually by the time students are in middle school they know that families, schools and other groups make rules that must be followed. Even peer groups may have rules. That doesn't always mean that students are happy with the rules, or that they always agree with others. It is not unusual for students to disagree with other students, teachers, or even their parents.

Part of becoming an adult is learning how to express your own ideas without becoming aggressive, violent, or offending anyone. Middle and high school students are also learning when to express their ideas, and when to stay silent even if they disagree with someone. There are times when it is best to keep your opinion to yourself.

Usually when people disagree with another person or a group of people they feel uncomfortable. Sometimes they might feel angry. Sometimes they might feel sad or worried or even embarrassed. It is important that students try to wait until they feel calm to talk about a problem or a disagreement.

When students are calm, they can begin to negotiate a disagreement. Negotiation means discussing thoughts, feelings and ideas, and deciding if rules can or should be changed. Negotiation also means listening to different ideas and points of view, even if you disagree with them. Usually if one person is willing to try to make a change, other people will also try to make a change. This is called compromise. It is smart to try to negotiate a disagreement when all the people involved have enough time to talk about it, and when they have a quiet, private place to talk.

Sometimes rules cannot be changed. Sometimes people have a very difficult time understanding a different point of view because they are certain that their ideas are right. Even though students don't always understand the reasons, some rules are in place to make sure everyone is safe, or because they are part of the law. If an adult or a teacher tells a student the rule cannot be changed, it is probably best to stop trying to negotiate with that person. Sometimes students must keep their opinions to themselves. Sometimes students have to follow rules even if they disagree with them.

I can try to negotiate with others when I disagree with them. I can relax first so I am calm. Sometimes I can compromise with another person when we talk in private and in a quiet place. I know some rules can't be changed. When a rule can't be changed I will try to keep my opinion to myself and follow the rule.

Negotiating with Others – Activity Sheet

Materials

- ❑ "Negotiating With Others" experiential story
- ❑ Negotiation Practice cards

Procedure

- ❑ Review "Negotiating With Others" experiential story.
- ❑ Allow students to select and read out loud a Negotiation Practice card.
- ❑ Ask the class if the card describes a "rule" or something that can be negotiated.
- ❑ Ask a volunteer to begin a negotiation by suggesting a compromise that would address the situation on the Negotiation Practice card.

Negotiation Practice cards

Directions: Copy on colored paper, laminate, and cut into cards.

You want to watch a game show on TV, but your sister wants to watch a movie.

Your best friend just got a new computer game you really wanted to try, but he doesn't want to share.

Your parent wants you to go mow your grandmother's lawn, but you want to watch TV.

Your neighbor says he will pay you $1 to walk his dog, but you think he should pay more.

You like wearing torn jeans to school, but it is against the dress code.

Your best friend wants to eat lunch with someone else.

Your friends want to go to the school basketball game, but you want to go swimming.

Your parents tell you they want you to come with them to the zoo; you think it's boring.

You like to do your homework after dinner; your dad thinks you should do it when you get home from school.

Your sister wants to get a cat; you want a dog.

Your math teacher wants you to show your work; you think it's a waste of time.

Your neighbor doesn't like it when your friends run on his front lawn when you play football after school.

You are watching a movie, but your brother wants to watch a basketball game instead.

Your family orders pepperoni pizza all the time; you like plain cheese.

Your best friend tells you he found the answers to tomorrow's science test.

Your parents want to repaint your room pink; you like blue.

QUEST Program II: Social Skills Curriculum for Middle School Students with Autism
© by JoEllen Cumpata and Susan Fell. Future Horizons, Inc.

QUEST Program II UPDATE!

Dear Parent,

This week your child has been working hard in QUEST Program II to master the skill of

Negotiating with Others

Together we have learned:

- What negotiation is and why it is important.

- Why differences of opinion and disagreements, even between friends, are normal.

- How to work through a disagreement with a friend or family member.

You can help your child learn more at home by:

- Practicing active problem solving in your home by following these steps when a disagreement occurs.

  1. Find a private place to talk.

  2. Listen to the other person's point of view.

  3. Explain your point of view calmly without shouting or name calling.

  4. Talk about ways the situation can be changed or improved.

  5. Decide what changes you should try.

- Listening and empathizing when your child discusses a disagreement they have had with another person, while resisting the temptation to offer solutions too quickly or "fix" the problem for your child.

- Helping your child consider the ways they can respond or problem solve with others. Role-play is a great way to do this.

Thanks for your help!

Problem Solving – Experiential Story

Friends, students, and adults don't always agree about everything. When people become angry or frustrated about their disagreements it can become a problem. When students have a problem they may shout, stamp their feet, look mad, pout, say mean things or tease each other. This is called being aggressive.

When students are angry at each other it is very hard to solve a problem. Sometimes angry students act aggressively and say or do things that are against school rules like throwing things, breaking things, or hurting other students. This can be dangerous. Sometimes angry students just feel bad inside and wish they could feel better.

Some students who have a problem with others don't do anything about it. Students might sulk, complain, or remain quiet. This is called being passive. When students are passive the problem is not usually solved and students will keep feeling uncomfortable about the problem.

When students don't solve their problems with other students, sometimes they feel so angry that they can no longer be friends. If students don't know how to solve problems they may have difficulty making or keeping friends.

If two or more students have a problem sometimes they can talk it out and figure out a way to solve it. This is called being assertive. Assertive students solve problems by talking them out. Solving problems can make students feel happy and relaxed again. Some students even become friends again when they solve a problem. To solve a problem in an assertive way students need to:

1. CALM DOWN - our brain doesn't work well when we are upset.

    *   Relax

    *   Breathe deeply

    *   Wait until you feel calm enough to talk

2. LISTEN AND TALK - we can't work it out unless we talk together.

    *   Ask for a good time to meet

    *   Find a quiet, private place

    *   Listen to the other person's point of view

    *   Tell your point of view

QUEST Program II: Social Skills Curriculum for Middle School Students with Autism
© by JoEllen Cumpata and Susan Fell. Future Horizons, Inc.

3. BRAINSTORM – everyone views the world a bit differently.

   - Talk about all the ways you can solve the problem

   - Think about which solutions would work

   - Agree on which solution to try

4. DECIDE - you might have to compromise, which means you may need to let others try some of their ideas.

   - Write down your agreement

   - Meet again if it is not working

All students have disagreements with other students or adults. Sometimes this can be a real problem. I may have disagreements sometimes, also. I can try to solve problems in an assertive way when I **calm down**, **listen and talk**, **brainstorm,** and **decide** on a way to fix the problem. This is one way to keep friends, be happy, and follow school rules.

Problem Solving – Activity Sheet

Materials

- ❑ "Problem-Solving" experiential story
- ❑ Problem-Solving Steps poster
- ❑ Problem-Solving scenario cards
- ❑ Passive, Aggressive, Assertive cards

Procedure

- ❑ Review "Problem-Solving" experiential story.
- ❑ Display the Problem-Solving Steps poster and review the steps to assertive problem solving.
- ❑ Lay the Passive, Aggressive, and Assertive cards face up on the table and describe each one to the students.
- ❑ Ask a student to choose a Problem Solving scenario card.
- ❑ Ask the student to describe an aggressive response to the situation on the card.
- ❑ Ask the student to describe a passive response to the situation on the card.
- ❑ Ask the student to describe an assertive response to the situation on the card.
- ❑ Discuss with the class.

Problem-Solving Steps poster

Directions: Enlarge and paste on poster board.

QUEST Program II: Social Skills Curriculum for Middle School Students with Autism
© by JoEllen Cumpata and Susan Fell. Future Horizons, Inc.

Problem-Solving Steps

1. **CALM DOWN - our brain doesn't work well when we are upset.**

   - Relax

   - Breathe deeply

   - Wait until you feel calm enough to talk

2. **LISTEN AND TALK - we can't work it out unless we talk together.**

   - Ask for a good time to meet

   - Find a quiet, private place

   - Listen to the other person's point of view

   - Tell your point of view

3. **BRAINSTORM – everyone views the world a bit differently.**

   - Talk about all the ways you can solve the problem

   - Think about which solutions would work

   - Agree on which solution to try

4. **DECIDE - you might have to compromise, which means you may need to let others try some of their ideas.**

   - Write down your agreement

   - Meet again if it is not working

Problem Solving scenario cards

Directions: Copy on colored paper, laminate, and cut into cards.

You want to go see a movie, but your friend just wants to stay home and play video games.

Your parent thinks you should take the trash out at 5 p.m.; you think you should decide on the time.

You want to do your math homework after dinner, but your parent wants you to do it now.

You want to sign up to go to the library at lunch, but your friend wants to go outside.

Your teacher thinks you should work as part of group, but you want to do your project alone.

Your parent thinks you should go to bed at 9 p.m.; you think you should be able to stay up later.

QUEST Program II: Social Skills Curriculum for Middle School Students with Autism
© by JoEllen Cumpata and Susan Fell. Future Horizons, Inc.

You want to swing on the swings at lunch, but other students are always using them.

You're sick of eating peanut butter and jelly for lunch, but your mother keeps giving it to you.

You want to read a book, but your brother keeps throwing a ball at you.

Your parent wants to take the whole family out to dinner, but your favorite TV show is on.

You want to ride your bike with friends, but your best friend wants to stay inside and read.

You overhear one of your friends saying something mean about you during lunch.

You want to go swimming in the park, but your sister doesn't want to go.

You really want a dog, but your parent says they are too much work.

You want to do your group project on dinosaurs, but the others in the group don't like that topic.

You would like to go bowling, but your friend says it's stupid.

Passive, Aggressive, Assertive cards

Directions: Copy each card on a different color of paper, laminate.

Passive

Not respecting yourself, voicing your opinion, or having your needs met

QUEST Program II: Social Skills Curriculum for Middle School Students with Autism
© by JoEllen Cumpata and Susan Fell. Future Horizons, Inc.

Agressive

Not respecting others, using verbal threats, name-calling, or physical violence

Assertive

Respecting yourself and others, problem solving, being willing to compromise

QUEST Program II UPDATE!

Dear Parent,

This week your child has been working hard in QUEST Program II to master the skill of

Problem Solving

Together we have learned and practiced:

- Effective problem solving steps

    1. Calm down - use the relaxation strategies we have learned

    2. Listen and talk - find a private, quiet place to discuss the situation

    3. Brainstorm – calmly discuss all possible solutions

    4. Decide – agree on which solutions you will try

- Three styles of problem solving: passive, aggressive, and assertive.

Throughout the year we will be using the problem-solving steps in QUEST Program II to help students work through any problems/concerns they have, and model effective problem-solving.

You can help your child practice at home by reminding them to relax, talk things out, and brainstorm when you disagree, or when they have a problem. Role-model this technique, e.g., "Seems like we are both too upset to talk about this now. Let's try again after dinner." or "Sounds like you were really mad at school today!" or "Let's think about all your choices."

Help your child decide on the best solution and check back with them in a day or two to see how it worked out.

Thanks for your help!

QUEST Program II: Social Skills Curriculum for Middle School Students with Autism
© by JoEllen Cumpata and Susan Fell. Future Horizons, Inc.

QUEST Program II Unit Two Understanding and Managing Emotions Unit Evaluation

Student Name _____ Date _____

Evaluator _____

We have just completed a unit in QUEST Program II on Understanding and Managing Emotions. Please fill out the rating scale below to assist us in determining how well your student has generalized the skills taught, and if you have noticed improvement in their level of skill over the past six weeks. Check all boxes that apply, below.

O=Often S=Sometimes N=Never I=Improvement   **How Often Skill Is Observed**

Skill	O	S	N	I
Distinguishing facial expression, body language and tone associated with emotions Recognize and associate smiles, frowns, eyebrow position, loud and soft voices, arm crossing, foot stamping, and other types of body language with appropriate emotion.				
Identifying uncomfortable emotions in self Verbalize statements indicating you are experiencing an uncomfortable emotion.				
Practicing relaxation techniques when feeling uncomfortable feelings Use deep breathing, counting to ten, taking a "time-out," retreating to your room or quiet space, using art, music, or other types of relaxation techniques when feeling uncomfortable.				
Using stress management strategies Use relaxation techniques, exercise, recreation, healthy eating, and other strategies. Talk over problems with an adult you trust.				

Comments _____

_____

_____

Thank you for your input!

Unit 3

Communication Skills

Goal

To learn, practice, and improve reciprocal communication skills

Objectives

➢ To recognize and appropriately interpret nonverbal forms of communication including gestures, facial expressions, and body language.

➢ To use greetings and choose topics of interest to initiate conversation.

➢ To maintain conversation by staying on topic and using appropriate listening skills.

➢ To use exit phrases and nonverbal communication to end a conversation.

➢ To understand how to join an ongoing conversation by using proximity, body language, eye contact, greetings, and topic maintenance.

➢ To recognize when a conversation has become uncomfortable, too lengthy or inappropriate, and practice suitable exit strategies.

QUEST Program II: Social Skills Curriculum for Middle School Students with Autism
© by JoEllen Cumpata and Susan Fell. Future Horizons, Inc.

Experiential Stories, Activities, and Parent Updates

Stories can be read by parents, teachers, or students. Often students gain a deeper understanding of skills when stories can be discussed in detail in a group setting. Asking students to summarize paragraphs, relate their personal experiences and complete activities are all effective ways to increase generalization of skills. Parent Updates provide additional ways to continue learning at home. The letter "A" denotes advanced sections appropriate for students in their second or third year of the program.

Topics included in this unit are:

1. Nonverbal Communication

2. Starting a Conversation

3. Keeping a Conversation Going

4. Ending a Conversation

5. Joining a Group Conversation - A

6. Exiting an Uncomfortable Conversation – A

Nonverbal Communication – Experiential Story

Words are one way students communicate and have conversation with others. Often middle school students also use body movements, gestures, facial expressions, touching, and voice tone to communicate with friends, teachers, or family members. This kind of communication doesn't use words and is called nonverbal communication.

Students may use gestures or body language to support what they are saying in words or to emphasize what they are feeling. Students might use gestures or body language by shrugging their shoulders, turning their head slightly to one side, clenching their fist or stamping their foot. All of the gestures and body language people use when talking add information to what the person is saying.

Facial expressions are another form of nonverbal communication. Students can show another person that they are confused, concerned, frightened, or excited, by the expression on their face.

Sometimes students touch another person when they are talking. Students may pat each other on the back, give a soft punch in the arm, or tap on the shoulder. Family members may hug each other. At school, students usually feel best if they have some space around them when they are in a group. Sometimes students may feel uncomfortable if another person touches them. Students usually touch only their closest friends.

Another way students use nonverbal communication is by using a loud or soft voice. This is called "voice tone." Voice tone can tell us if someone is angry, sad, in a hurry, or excited.

Students can pay close attention to gestures, body language, facial expressions, touching, and voice tone when they talk or listen to others. Noticing these things can give students extra information. When another person is talking loud, fast, and moving around a lot, it might mean that they are excited, in a hurry or even late. When students look at the floor, keep their hands in their pockets and talk quietly, it might mean that they are feeling sad, shy, or upset.

I can try to pay close attention to nonverbal communication when I am talking or listening to another person. I can try to be aware of the nonverbal communication I am using. When I pay close attention to the nonverbal communication between myself and the people I talk with, I can get more information, and communicate more clearly to others.

QUEST Program II: Social Skills Curriculum for Middle School Students with Autism
© by JoEllen Cumpata and Susan Fell. Future Horizons, Inc.

Nonverbal Communication – Activity Sheet

Materials

- ❑ "Nonverbal Communication" experiential story
- ❑ Nonverbal Communication examples cards

Procedure

- ❑ Read "Nonverbal Communication" experiential story.
- ❑ Show students one Nonverbal Communication examples card.
- ❑ Ask students to identify gestures, body language and facial expressions they see on the card.
- ❑ Discuss what other information we learn about the person from noticing the nonverbal communication.

Nonverbal Communication Examples cards

Directions: Copy on colored paper, laminate, and cut into cards.
Copy with or without descriptor words attached.

Interested

Bored

Angry

Happy

QUEST Program II: Social Skills Curriculum for Middle School Students with Autism
© by JoEllen Cumpata and Susan Fell. Future Horizons, Inc.

Frustrated

Excited

Sad

Worried

Nonverbal Communication – Activity Sheet

Materials

- ❑ "Nonverbal Communication" experiential story
- ❑ Nonverbal Communication Scenarios cards

Procedure

- ❑ Read "Nonverbal Communication" experiential story.
- ❑ Turn Nonverbal Communication Scenarios cards face down on table.
- ❑ Ask one student to choose a card and read it out loud to the group.
- ❑ Ask students to demonstrate gestures, body language and facial expressions they might have if they had the experience on the card.
- ❑ Ask for student feedback.

Nonverbal Communication Scenarios cards

Directions: Copy on colored paper, laminate, and cut into cards.

QUEST Program II: Social Skills Curriculum for Middle School Students with Autism
© by JoEllen Cumpata and Susan Fell. Future Horizons, Inc.

You have too much homework.

You were invited to a friend's birthday party.

Your Dad is going into the hospital for an operation.

The science lab you are going to work on is really fascinating!

You did the same science lab last year and you think it is boring.

Your group in social studies is talking too much and not doing their work.

You are going to ask a friend if they want to see a movie with you this weekend.

You have a substitute teacher in math and you don't understand the assignment.

Your mother is angry with you because you broke her favorite lamp.

Your dog ran away.

You get an A+ on your social studies test.

Another student calls you a bad name.

Your physical education teacher announces that you will be learning how to dive in swimming today.

You fall on the playground, rip your pants, and cut your knee.

Your parents tell you that they are adopting a new dog.

QUEST Program II: Social Skills Curriculum for Middle School Students with Autism
© by JoEllen Cumpata and Susan Fell. Future Horizons, Inc.

QUEST Program II UPDATE!

Dear Parent,

This week your child has been working hard in QUEST Program II to master the skill of

Understanding Nonverbal Communication

Together we have learned and practiced:

- Ways to use gestures, facial expressions, and voice tone to improve our personal communication.

- Ways to notice body language in others to gain information.

You can help your child practice at home by:

- Noticing body language in others and verbalizing its possible meaning to your child, e.g., "That salesman has his arms crossed and a frown on his face. He looks angry. Let's go ask that other salesperson about the shoes. She has a smile on her face and looks happy." or "Grandpa is slouching and has his head in his hands. He looks bored. Why don't you ask him if he wants to play chess?"

- Encouraging your child to become more aware of his or her own body language, e.g., "By the big smile on your face, I can tell you are happy about the movie we've selected." or "When you didn't look up or smile, I think Sara thought you didn't want to be friends."

Thanks for your help!

Starting a Conversation – Experiential Story

Middle school students often have conversations throughout their day. A conversation is when two or more people talk to each other about something they have in common, or something they are interested in. Talking together through conversation is one way students make and keep friends. Students can have conversations with other students, family members, teachers, and even people they don't know very well.

When a student wants to start a conversation with another student they need to walk up to the student and stand an arm's length away. They also need to look at the person's face and have good eye contact. This lets the other person know that a conversation might happen. When the other person is paying attention, students can start a conversation by using a greeting. Students can say, "Hello," "Hi," or "How are you?" before beginning a conversation.

After students use a greeting they usually talk about something they have in common. This means something they both know a lot about, something they both like or have experienced. Family members might talk about their pet, trips they have taken, or a TV show they have just watched. Students can also talk about what they have in common. Sometimes this might be sports or activities they enjoy, classes they share, TV shows, video games or movies, or another interest both students have.

If you are starting a conversation with someone you don't know very well you might make a comment about the weather, or talk about something that is going on in your school or community.

Having conversations can be fun and interesting. Starting a conversation is a great way to be friendly. I can start conversations too by:

- Standing an arm's length away

- Using good eye contact

- Greeting someone

- Talking about things we have in common

I can talk and be friendly with family members, teachers, and other students at school.

QUEST Program II: Social Skills Curriculum for Middle School Students with Autism
© by JoEllen Cumpata and Susan Fell. Future Horizons, Inc.

Starting a Conversation – Activity Sheet

Materials

- ❑ "Starting a Conversation" experiential story
- ❑ What Do They Have in Common poster
- ❑ Conversation cards
- ❑ Sticky poster tack

Procedure

- ❑ Read "Starting a Conversation" experiential story.
- ❑ Review what "having something in common" means.
- ❑ Place Conversation cards right-side up on the table.
- ❑ Ask one student to select a card and place it on the left side of the What Do They Have in Common poster, using poster tack.
- ❑ Ask a second student to select another card that relates to the first and place it on the right side of the poster (follow arrow).
- ❑ Remind students about the conversation rules: eye contact, arm's-length away, using greetings, and talking about things we have in common.
- ❑ Ask students to look at the cards they selected and start a conversation about their card.
- ❑ Ask the group to compliment presenters and make suggestions for improvement.
- ❑ Repeat activity with other students until all pictures have been used.

What Do They Have In Common poster

Directions: Enlarge and paste on poster board, laminate.

Conversation cards

Directions: Enlarge and copy pictures below on colored paper,
cut into squares, and laminate.

What Do They Have In Common?

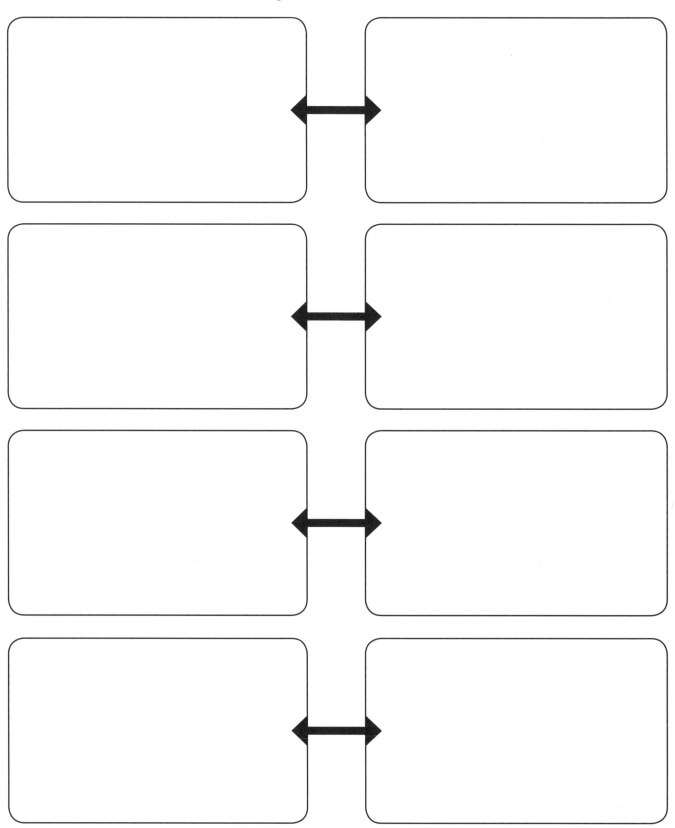

Conversation cards

Conversation cards

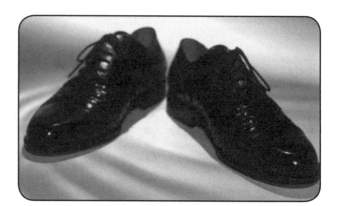

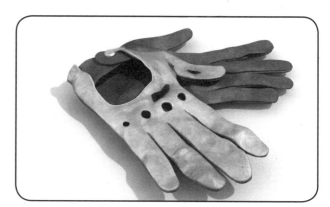

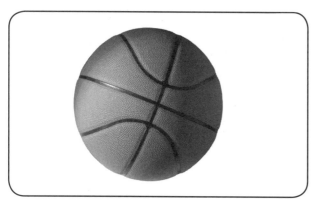

QUEST Program II: Social Skills Curriculum for Middle School Students with Autism
© by JoEllen Cumpata and Susan Fell. Future Horizons, Inc.

Conversation cards

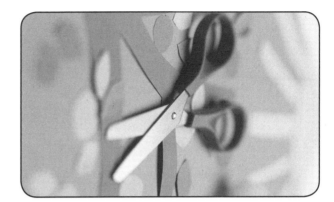

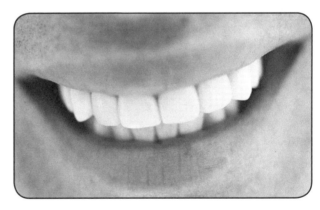

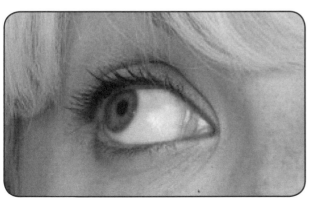

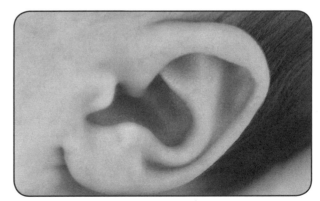

Starting a Conversation – Activity Sheet

Materials

- ❑ "Starting a Conversation" experiential story
- ❑ Student Interests cards

Procedure

- ❑ Read "Starting a Conversation" experiential story.
- ❑ Review what "having something in common" means.
- ❑ Hold up one of the Student Interests cards for all to view.
- ❑ Ask students to think about what they might have in common with the student in the picture.
- ❑ Have a volunteer give an example of a statement they could use to start a conversation with the person in the picture.
- ❑ Repeat activity with other students until all pictures have been used.

Student Interests cards

Directions: Enlarge and copy Student Interests pictures on colored paper, cut into squares, and laminate.

QUEST Program II: Social Skills Curriculum for Middle School Students with Autism
© by JoEllen Cumpata and Susan Fell. Future Horizons, Inc.

Student Interest cards

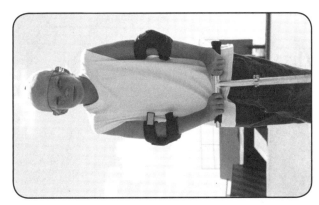

Student Interest cards

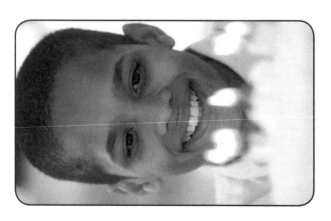 

QUEST Program II: Social Skills Curriculum for Middle School Students with Autism
© by JoEllen Cumpata and Susan Fell. Future Horizons, Inc.

Student Interest cards

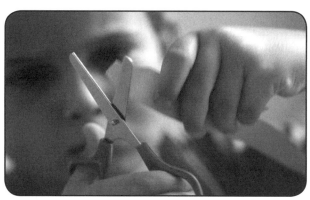

QUEST Program II UPDATE!

Dear Parent,

This week your child has been working hard in QUEST Program II to master the skill of

Starting a Conversation

Together we have learned and practiced:

- Using a proper greeting before starting a conversation.

- Using correct body language and eye contact during conversation.

- Discussing something you have in common with another student.

You can help your child practice at home by:

- Asking your child to tell you one fun thing that happened at school each day.

- Reminding your child to stand approximately one arm's-length away and use good eye contact during conversation with you.

- Suggesting conversational topics that people have in common, e.g., "It's fun to talk about sports with Grandpa. You both really enjoy basketball." or "I bet your cousin would like to talk with you about your new video game. She really enjoys them also." or "I think Jason from down the street also enjoys drawing cartoons. Maybe you could ask him what his favorite drawing is."

Thanks for your help!

Keeping a Conversation Going – Experiential Story

When students start a conversation they usually want to keep it going for a few minutes or longer. Keeping a conversation going lets others know that we are interested in what they have to say, and that we want to be friendly. If a conversation is started and we walk away or don't keep it going, other students may think that we are not friendly or that we are not interested in what they have to say.

Some conversations are very short. Students need to keep conversations short if they are in a hurry or if the other person has other things to do. Conversations should be short at school between classes because students are in a hurry to get to their next class. Students can have longer conversations at school when they and the other person both have more time to talk, like during lunch.

When students begin a conversation they stand an arm's-length away, look at the other person's eyes and use a greeting. To keep a conversation going, students need to think about what they have in common or what might be interesting about what the other person is saying.

To keep a conversation going students should listen to the other person and either ask a question or make a comment about what the person has said. Students also need to listen closely to what the other person says and make sure they say something that is related.

Sometimes students respond to conversation by using only one word like "yes," "no," or "maybe." When students use only one word in a conversation it is hard to keep the conversation going.

When students have conversation they listen, talk, listen and talk to one another. Having conversation is something like a game of ping-pong. One student speaks while another listens, then the other student speaks. Usually each person says one or two sentences before they let the other person speak and they listen.

I can try keeping a conversation going by listening, saying something related and trying not to answer with only one word. I can say one or two things about the topic and then listen to what the other person has to say. When I have conversations with other students or teachers they will know that I am interested and friendly.

Keeping a Conversation Going – Activity Sheet

Materials

- ❑ "Keeping a Conversation Going" experiential story
- ❑ Conversation cards from Starting a Conversation activity
- ❑ Ball of yarn

Procedure

- ❑ Read "Keeping a Conversation Going" experiential story.
- ❑ Select one of the Conversation cards.
- ❑ Show picture to the group and explain that students will be keeping a conversation about that card going as long as possible.
- ❑ Hold the end of the yarn and make a comment about the card. Roll yarn to a student. Ask that student to make a comment or ask a question about the card which is related to the statement you made.
- ❑ Continue to roll the yarn and comment using related comments and questions, forming a "conversation web" with the yarn.

QUEST Program II: Social Skills Curriculum for Middle School Students with Autism
© by JoEllen Cumpata and Susan Fell. Future Horizons, Inc.

QUEST Program II UPDATE!

Dear Parent,

This week your child has been working hard in QUEST Program II to master the skill of

Keeping a Conversation Going

Together we have learned and practiced:

- Using good eye contact and body language during conversation

- Saying one or two sentences at a time

- Listening to what the other person is saying

- Responding with a statement, question, or comment that is on topic

- Avoiding conversation stoppers like one-word answers

- Taking turns talking

You can help your child practice at home by:

- Greeting your child each evening and asking them to tell you one thing that happened to them that day. Sharing something that happened to you and seeing how long you both can keep the conversation going

- Suggesting possible conversation topics to your child right before peer or family social events

- Reminding your child to face you, use good eye contact, and stay on topic when you have conversation at home

- Asking your child what "ping-pong" has to do with conversation

Thanks for your help!

Ending a Conversation – Experiential Story

All conversations have to end sometime. Students cannot talk to each other all day. Sometimes students run out of things to say. Sometimes the conversation becomes boring. Sometimes students want to keep talking, but they need to get to class, go to lunch or go somewhere else, or listen to their teacher.

When students want to end a conversation it is important that they do it in a friendly way. If a student just stops talking and walks away from the other student without ending the conversation properly, others may think that they are not friendly or not interested.

Students can let others know that they want to end a conversation in a friendly way by using nonverbal communication like body language, tone or eye contact, and by using words. If students are sitting and want to end a conversation, they can stand up to let the other person know that the conversation is ending. If students are standing they can begin to move away from each other to end the conversation. Students can also glance at a clock or their watch to let others know that they need to end the conversation.

Another way to end a conversation is by using friendly words. Students can say, "Well, I need to go now," "It was nice talking to you," or even, "I'm late!" if they need to end a conversation. Using a goodbye statement is always a friendly way to end a conversation. Goodbye statements are words like "Bye," "So long," or "See you later."

During conversation, it is important to pay attention to the other people talking to know when the conversation may be ending. Students can watch the body language and listen to statements others make to know when a conversation is ending.

I can try not to walk away from a conversation until I have used friendly body language or words to end a conversation. I can also try to watch the body language of other people during conversation and listen for goodbye statements so I will know when the conversation is ending. When I end my conversations in friendly ways, others will look forward to having conversations with me again and know I am friendly and interested.

QUEST Program II: Social Skills Curriculum for Middle School Students with Autism
© by JoEllen Cumpata and Susan Fell. Future Horizons, Inc.

Ending a Conversation – Activity Sheet

Materials

- ❑ "Ending a Conversation" experiential story
- ❑ Conversation Topics cards

Procedure

- ❑ Read "Ending a Conversation" experiential story.
- ❑ Select a Conversation Topics card and read it to the group.
- ❑ Select one or more students to have a conversation with.
- ❑ Ask for one volunteer to end the conversation.
- ❑ Initiate a conversation with students about the topic.
- ❑ After student has ended conversation, discuss what body language or words were used.

Conversation Topics cards

Directions: Copy on colored paper, laminate, and cut into cards.

I saw a great football game last night on TV.

My family went out of town last weekend.

I tried snow skiing for the first time.

Video games are fun.

I think it is going to snow today.

Looks like we are going to get a storm today.

We have a test today.

I have too much homework.

I'm excited about vacation.

I like to watch movies.

We just got a new puppy.

Our cat ran away from home.

I like *The Lord of the Rings* movies.

I like playing video games.

My birthday is next week.

My dad is sick.

I have to go to the dentist.

We are swimming in PE today.

My grandpa is in the hospital.

My cousin is coming to visit.

I really like to listen to rap music.

I'm trying out for the basketball team.

We might sell our house.

We just got a new car.

QUEST Program II UPDATE!

Dear Parent,

This week your child has been working hard in QUEST Program II to master the skill of

Ending a Conversation

Together we have learned:

- How to recognize when a conversation should end

- How to use nonverbal communication to end a conversation (i.e., checking your watch, standing up, starting to walk away)

- How to use friendly words to end a conversation

You can help your child practice at home by:

- Praising them when they end a conversation appropriately, e.g., "I noticed that you listened to grandpa very carefully, and when he was done talking you said you needed to do your homework. This was a good way to end the conversation."

- Making suggestions in private if your child has not ended a conversation appropriately, e.g., "When Patty tried to talk to you in the mall, you just walked away. She probably thought you didn't like her. Next time you may want to say, 'It was nice seeing you.' before you walk away." or "I know we were in a hurry today when Mr. Smith tried to talk with you, but he might think you are not friendly if you just walk away. What could you say next time, to let him know we are in a hurry and don't have time to talk?"

Thanks for your help!

Joining a Group Conversation – Experiential Story

Most students like to be friendly and talk to other students. Often students are friends with more than one other student. It is not unusual for many students to have a conversation together while in a group.

Often when students are talking in a group, more than one person may be talking at a time. Students may be laughing, moving about, and even walking away from the group at different times. Sometimes a group of students may even be talking about two or three different things in the same group.

When students are standing together and talking, it is okay for other students to join in the conversation. It is important for students to follow these three steps when joining in a group conversation:

- Move toward the group and stand about an arm's-length away from one or two other students. When a student walks up to a group and stands close to other students, they know he or she wants to be a part of the group.

- Look at one of the students who is talking and smile. This lets the others know you are friendly and want to join in the conversation.

- Use a greeting when there is a break in the conversation, and say something that is "on topic" with the discussion. "On topic" means that it relates to the conversation. When students wait until the others have stopped talking, they are being polite and not interrupting. When students stay on topic, the others in the group know that they are listening and find the topic interesting.

It can be fun and interesting to join in a group conversation. Having group conversations is one way to make friends in middle school. Sometimes students are talking about more than one topic in a group.

I can join in group conversations and make friends when I move toward a group of students, stand an arm's-length away, look at the student who is talking and smile, use a greeting, and stay on topic.

QUEST Program II: Social Skills Curriculum for Middle School Students with Autism
© by JoEllen Cumpata and Susan Fell. Future Horizons, Inc.

Joining a Group Conversation – Activity Sheet

Materials

- ❑ "Joining a Group Conversation" experiential story
- ❑ Joining a Group Conversation poster
- ❑ Conversation Topics cards

Procedure

- ❑ Read "Joining a Group Conversation" experiential story.
- ❑ Display Joining a Group Conversation poster and discuss rules listed on poster.
- ❑ Select one or two Conversation Topics cards and read to the group.
- ❑ Select three or more students to have a group conversation.
- ❑ Ask for one volunteer to attempt to join the conversation.
- ❑ Ask the class to discuss what the student did well and what could be improved upon.

Joining a Group Conversation poster

Directions: Enlarge and paste on poster board.

Joining a Group Conversation

Walk near the group and make eye contact.

Smile and use a greeting.

Wait for a break in the conversation.

Stay on topic.

QUEST Program II UPDATE!

Dear Parent,
This week your child has been working hard in QUEST Program II to master the skill of

Joining a Group Conversation

Together we have learned:

- How to join a conversation in progress

- Group conversations often involve many topics being discussed at the same time.

You can help your child practice at home by:

- Encouraging your child to join group conversations at family functions and other social events, e.g., "I see your cousins Jake, Patty, and Brian over there talking together. Why don't you walk on over and join their conversation?" or "It looks like the boys on the team are having a discussion under the tree. I bet they are talking about the game. Why don't you join them?"

- Commenting when you notice your child properly join a group conversation, e.g., "Paul, it was nice how you greeted Sara and Luke when you joined in on their conversation." or "Andrew, I heard you talking with the other students at the school dance. Sounded like all the boys were interested in video games too."

Thanks for your help!

Exiting an Uncomfortable Conversation – Experiential Story

Most students enjoy having conversations with others. Once in a while a student may start to feel awkward or uncomfortable when they are having a conversation. Students may feel uncomfortable when they are talking with their friends, students from their school, or students that they do not know.

Students do not always talk about topics that are appropriate or kind. Students may talk about inappropriate things they have seen on the Internet, like violent or adult-only Web sites. Students may say hurtful things, or gossip about other students. They also may talk about things that are against school rules, or against the law, like drinking alcohol, skipping school, destroying property, or stealing.

When students are in a group that is having this type of conversation they may feel uncomfortable or awkward because they don't want to do what the others are planning, or they don't want to talk about the topic because it is inappropriate.

Students can try to change the topic when it becomes uncomfortable. One way to change the topic is by letting others know you don't want to talk about the topic anymore, and then saying one or two sentences about a more appropriate topic. Sometimes students do not want to change the topic. It is important for students to leave a conversation if they feel uncomfortable with the topic.

When a student wants to leave this type of conversation, they can use a "quick exit line" like, "I've got to go. See you," "I'd better be going," or "See you later." After using the quick exit line, students can walk away from the group.

Sometimes students may have friends over who start an uncomfortable or inappropriate conversation. If this happens, it is OK to tell these students that you are not allowed to talk about those things in your home, and change the topic. Students who do not want to change the topic may be asked to go home.

It is fun and interesting to have conversations. Sometimes conversations become inappropriate or awkward. It is important to use a "quick exit line" when conversations become uncomfortable. When I use a quick exit line and walk away, I can be comfortable and follow rules.

QUEST Program II: Social Skills Curriculum for Middle School Students with Autism
© by JoEllen Cumpata and Susan Fell. Future Horizons, Inc.

Exiting an Uncomfortable Conversation – Activity Sheet

Materials

- ❑ "Exiting an Uncomfortable Conversation" experiential story
- ❑ Uncomfortable Conversation cards
- ❑ Quick Exit Line cards

Procedure

- ❑ Read "Exiting an Uncomfortable Conversation" experiential story.
- ❑ Select an Uncomfortable Conversation card and read to the group.
- ❑ Select one or more students to participate in a conversation.
- ❑ Ask for one volunteer to exit the conversation.
- ❑ Suggest students select a Quick Exit Line card if they have difficulty ending the conversation.
- ❑ After the student has ended conversation, discuss what body language or words were used.

Uncomfortable Conversation cards

Directions: Copy on colored paper, laminate, and cut into cards.

Quick Exit Line cards

Directions: Copy on colored paper, laminate, and cut into cards.

I found out about this website where you can look at R-rated movies.

My friend told me that Eric has some cigarettes.

I didn't do my homework. Anybody want to skip class?

Yesterday I stole some candy from the store.

John's such a baby.

I think Mrs. Smith is such an idiot. Let's hide her grade book.

John's parents are out of town. Let's egg his house after school today.

I know this kid that keeps lots of money in his locker.

Gotta go!

Wow, I'm late!

I forgot something in my locker.

See you later.

I'm not interested. Anyone going to the game?

Let's not talk about him.

I don't want to talk about this anymore.

I've got to get home early today.

QUEST Program II UPDATE!

Dear Parent,

This week your child has been working hard in QUEST Program II to master the skill of

Exiting an Uncomfortable Conversation

Together we have learned:

- How to recognize an uncomfortable conversation, e.g., students are gossiping or talking about something that is against school rules.

- Why it is sometimes important to quickly leave a group when the conversation becomes uncomfortable.

- How to use a "quick exit" line when the conversation becomes uncomfortable.

You can help your child practice at home by:

- Discussing some possible scenarios your child could face, and role-playing an effective response, e.g., "I'll pretend I'm Eric. I'll start talking about cheating on the next test. Show me how you would use a quick exit line to get out of the conversation." or "Your sister and I will pretend we are talking about going to a party without telling our parents. Show me what you would say."

- Modeling appropriate responses when your child's friends are gossiping or talking about uncomfortable topics, e.g., "Janie, we don't talk about people that way. You will need to go home if I hear it again." or "Pete, we don't allow that type of discussion in our home. Pick something else to talk about."

Thanks for your help!

QUEST Program II: Social Skills Curriculum for Middle School Students with Autism
© by JoEllen Cumpata and Susan Fell. Future Horizons, Inc.

Communication Skills Unit Review

Materials

- ❑ Conversation Rules poster
- ❑ Conversation Topics cards from Ending a Conversation activity
- ❑ Conversation Rating Sheet for each student
- ❑ Pencils

Procedure

- ❑ Display Conversation Rules poster and communication skills previously taught and practiced.
- ❑ Place Conversation Topics cards upside down on table.
- ❑ Select one Conversation Topics card.
- ❑ Using topic on card, demonstrate strong and weak communication skills.
- ❑ Hand out Conversation Rating Sheet to each student.
- ❑ Ask students to observe and rate speakers on eye contact, distance, topic, and ending the conversation.
- ❑ Discuss
- ❑ Ask for two or more student volunteers to demonstrate a conversation.
- ❑ Have students rate each other.
- ❑ Discuss

Conversation Rules poster

Directions: Enlarge and paste on poster board.

Conversation Rules

- Stand an arm's-length away, use good eye contact and smile.

- Use a greeting.

- Talk about what you have in common.

- Stay on topic.

- Play verbal "ping-pong."

- Use a friendly good-bye statement.

QUEST Program II: Social Skills Curriculum for Middle School Students with Autism
© by JoEllen Cumpata and Susan Fell. Future Horizons, Inc.

Conversation Rating Sheet

Watch the person talking and rate them below.

	YES	NO
Do they have good eye contact?	☐	☐
Did they use a greeting?	☐	☐
Are they standing about one arm's-length away from the other person?	☐	☐
Did they choose a topic that they both have in common?	☐	☐
Did they play verbal ping-pong?	☐	☐
Did they end the conversation appropriately?	☐	☐

Do you have any suggestions to improve this conversation?

_____

_____

QUEST Program II Unit Three - Communication Skills
Unit Evaluation

Student Name _____ Date _____

Evaluator _____

We have just completed a unit in QUEST Program II on Communication Skills. Please fill out the rating scale below to assist us in determining how well your student has generalized the skills taught, and if you have noticed improvement in their level of skill over the past six weeks. Check all boxes that apply below.

O=Often S=Sometimes N=Never I=Improvement   **How Often Skill Is Observed**

Skill	O	S	N	I
Notice and interpret nonverbal communication Interpret body language, gestures appropriately. Stand arm's-length away from others. Read facial expressions accurately and use appropriately.				
Start a conversation with others without prompts Initiate conversations with friends and family. Use greetings and choose topics they have in common with peers/family.				
End a conversation Use body language of glancing at watch or clock, rising from chair, picking up books or moving toward door when ending a conversation. Use friendly good-bye statements, like, "I've got to go now." or "See you later." when ending conversation.				
Join ongoing conversations appropriately Stand on the perimeter of a group and greet them to join a conversation. Avoid interrupting others or speaking off topic.				
Exit uncomfortable conversations Is able to recognize when a conversation is becoming uncomfortable. Uses quick exit lines like, "I'm late." or "I'm not interested, got to go." to leave an uncomfortable conversation.				

Comments_____

Thank you for your input!

Unit 4

Making Friends and Interacting with Peers

Goal

To improve peer interaction skills

Objectives

- ➢ To understand and appreciate the importance of friendship.

- ➢ To learn and practice ways to initiate friendships with peers at school and in other settings.

- ➢ To appreciate the importance of socializing outside of school, and to understand how social engagements with friends are arranged.

- ➢ To learn and practice appropriate telephone use when making social arrangements with friends.

- ➢ To appreciate the necessity for modesty when around peers, and practice responses to uncomfortable situations involving modesty.

- ➢ To understand the concepts of teasing, gossiping, and bullying, recognize the difference between friendly and mean teasing, and practice effective responses to teasing, gossiping, and bullying.

- ➢ To demonstrate an understanding of the concept of peer pressure, and to practice assertiveness skills.

- ➢ To appreciate the opportunities for peer friendship-making offered during after-school activities.

- ➢ To understand adolescent peer relationship norms, including the concept of dating.

QUEST Program II: Social Skills Curriculum for Middle School Students with Autism
© by JoEllen Cumpata and Susan Fell. Future Horizons, Inc.

Experiential Stories, Activities, and Parent Updates

Stories can be read by parents, teachers or students. Often students gain a deeper understanding of skills when stories can be discussed in detail in a group setting. Asking students to summarize paragraphs, relate their personal experiences, and complete activities are all effective ways to increase generalization of skills. Parent Updates provide additional ways to continue learning at home. The letter "A" denotes advanced sections appropriate for students in their second or third year of the program.

Topics included in this unit are:

1. Friends are Important

2. Making and Keeping Friends

3. Making Plans with Friends

4. Using the Telephone

5. Modesty

6. Recognizing and Dealing with Gossiping, Bullying and Teasing

7. Resisting Peer Pressure - A

8. Participating in an After-School Activity - A

9. Dating – A

Friends Are Important – Experiential Story

Some students have lots of friends, some students don't. It is OK to have lots of friends and it is also OK to have just a few friends. Some students like to spend time alone at home, and aren't used to spending time with friends at school.

In school, many students spend time working on schoolwork, talking, and laughing with each other. Students spend time together in class, at lunch, and in the halls. When students have friends at school it makes the day more enjoyable and interesting.

Usually students choose friends who share their interests and have things in common. Students can be friends with other boys or girls. Friends are often in the same grade, but many students also have friends in different grades and at different schools.

Friends can help with assignments in class, tell jokes during lunch, discuss interesting books and movies, and play games together. Some friends like to move around a lot, play outside games and sports, and make a lot of noise. Some friends are more quiet and prefer to play inside, use the computer, read books or magazines, or watch the television. Usually students choose friends who like to do the same things, and like to talk about the same things.

While friends usually have fun together, they don't always agree with each other or get along. Sometimes friends who spend time together disagree or even have an argument. They might disagree about what game to play, or which other friends to be with, or something else. Disagreements with friends can feel uncomfortable, but it is normal for friends to disagree and argue sometimes. When friends argue, they might spend a little time apart but usually friends want to talk about their disagreement and work it out. Then they can be friends again.

It is nice to have a few friends or a lot of friends. I can have friends at school who like to do the same kinds of things that I do. When I disagree or argue with friends I can talk about it and work it out. Friends can make life more interesting and fun.

QUEST Program II: Social Skills Curriculum for Middle School Students with Autism
© by JoEllen Cumpata and Susan Fell. Future Horizons, Inc.

Friends Are Important – Activity Sheet

Materials

- ❑ "Friends Are Important" experiential story
- ❑ My Friendship Circle handouts
- ❑ My Friendship Circle Pictures handouts
- ❑ Glue sticks
- ❑ Scissors
- ❑ Pencils/Pens

Procedure

- ❑ Read "Friends Are Important" experiential story.
- ❑ Pass out a My Friendship Circle handout and My Friendship Circle Pictures handout to each student.
- ❑ Pair students and ask each team to complete a My Friendship Circle handout for both team members.
- ❑ Ask students to write names of family members, friends, and those they would like as friends in the appropriate section of their circle.
- ❑ Ask students to select pictures that illustrate activities they do or would like to do with their friends and glue in the appropriate section of their circle.
- ❑ Encourage teamwork and cooperation. Suggest one student cuts pictures while other pastes, etc.

Additional Activity

- ❑ Students can share with the group their reasons for selecting certain students or pictures as part of their My Friendship Circle project when they complete their weekly report.

My Friendship Circle

Think about people you know and fill in the friendship circle below. Cut out pictures from the My Friendship Circle Pictures handout, or draw things you like to do together within the circle. Be ready to talk about your friends and the things you like to do together, or the things you would like to try with your friends.

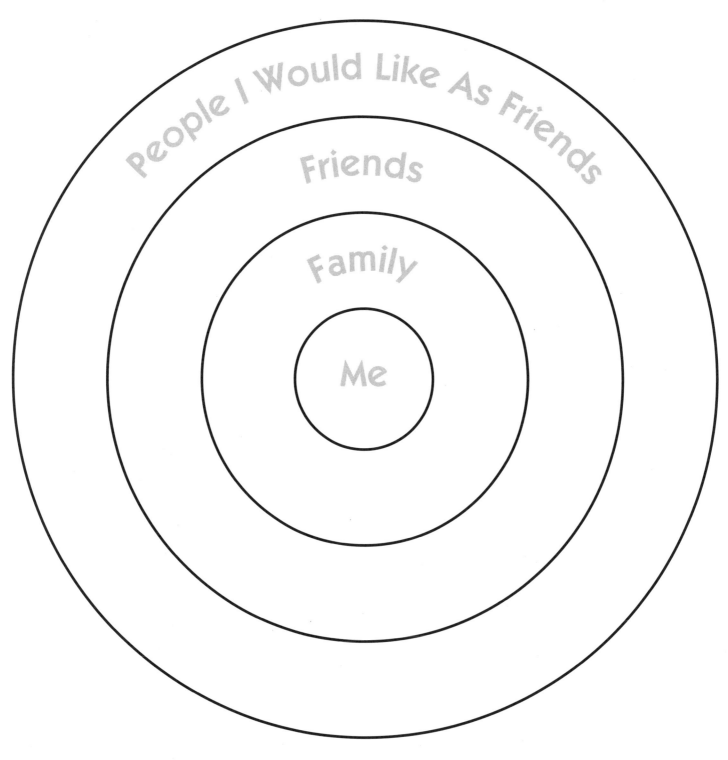

QUEST Program II: Social Skills Curriculum for Middle School Students with Autism
© by JoEllen Cumpata and Susan Fell. Future Horizons, Inc.

My Friendship Circle Pictures

QUEST Program II UPDATE!

Dear Parent,

This week your child has been working hard in QUEST Program II to master the skill of

The Importance of Friendship

Together we have:

- Learned why it is important to make and keep friends.

- Discussed truths and myths about friendship.

- Identified current friends and discussed other students who might be good choices as friends.

- Brainstormed appropriate social activities for middle school students.

- Talked about misunderstandings between friends, discussed why they are normal and what to do about them.

You can help your child practice new skills at home by:

- Learning more about your child's friends, and helping them learn more about their friends, e.g., "Tell me a bit more about Justin's family." or "Does your friend Sara also like reading?" or "Why don't you ask Pete what he did over the holiday break?"

- Helping your child think about possible social activities they could participate in with friends, or about things they have in common with their peers, e.g., "I know you really enjoy painting pottery, do you think Ellen would also like it?" or "I saw how much fun you had playing your new basketball video game, I wonder if a few of your friends might like to join you?" or "I'll bet Nicholas would really like to see your collection."

Thanks for your help!

QUEST Program II: Social Skills Curriculum for Middle School Students with Autism
© by JoEllen Cumpata and Susan Fell. Future Horizons, Inc.

Making and Keeping Friends – Experiential Story

In middle and high school, students often have many different classes and many different teachers. Sometimes students are in classes with their friends, sometimes they are not. School is a great place to make new friends. Having friends at school and in classes can make school more fun and interesting.

There are things students can do to make new friends. Students can make friends by greeting each other, making conversation, talking about things they have in common, walking together in the halls, or having lunch together, and even doing fun things outside of school.

When students greet each other in class, they need to make sure the class has not started yet. It is helpful to introduce yourself to people you do not know when you are greeting them.

Until students know each other well it might be difficult to know what they have in common. Some things new friends usually talk about are teachers, classes, homework, music, television and movies, video games, and even what the weather is like outside. These are all things that most students have in common.

Students can keep new friends by talking together each day in class, walking together in the halls, eating lunch together and making plans to get together after school. When new friends spend more time together, they know that they want to keep the friendship happening. When friends spend less time together, they may think that they do not have much in common, or that they are not interested in being better friends.

I can make new friends in school. Having friends in my classes makes them more fun and interesting. I can make new friends when I introduce myself, use a greeting, talk about things we have in common, and spend time together.

Making and Keeping Friends – Activity Sheet

Materials

- ❏ "Making and Keeping Friends" experiential story for each student
- ❏ Brown paper lunch bags
- ❏ Recreational Activity Icons handouts
- ❏ Glue sticks
- ❏ Scissors
- ❏ Crayons/Markers

Procedure

- ❏ Read "Making and Keeping Friends" experiential story.
- ❏ Hold up one of the Recreational Activity Icons handouts.
- ❏ Ask students what an icon is, and discuss what each could represent.
- ❏ Ask each student to design a paper bag hand-puppet that represents them.
- ❏ Ask each student to paste at least two icons from the handouts on the back of their paper bag puppet. These icons should represent things they enjoy doing or things they would like to try.
- ❏ Ask students to write the names of current friends, and students they would like to know better on the back of their puppet.
- ❏ Pair students and ask each pair to create a puppet skit to demonstrate one way to make a new friend.
- ❏ Act out skits for the group.

Recreational Activity Icons

Directions: Think about what these pictures represent and what you like to do in your free time. Cut out a few pictures that represent your interests and glue them on your paper bag puppet.

Recreational Activity Icons

Directions: Think about what these pictures represent and what you like to do in your free time. Cut out a few pictures that represent your interests and glue them on your paper bag puppet.

QUEST Program II: Social Skills Curriculum for Middle School Students with Autism
© by JoEllen Cumpata and Susan Fell. Future Horizons, Inc.

Making and Keeping Friends – Activity Sheet

Materials

- ❑ "Making and Keeping Friends" experiential story
- ❑ Making Friends poster
- ❑ Making Friends cards

Procedure

- ❑ Read "Making and Keeping Friends" experiential story.
- ❑ Display Making Friends poster and review steps students can take to make a new friend.
- ❑ Place Making Friends cards upside down on the table.
- ❑ Ask one student to choose a card and read it aloud.
- ❑ Ask students to describe how they might begin a friendship with the student on the card by discussing something they have in common.
- ❑ Discuss.

Making Friends poster

Directions: Enlarge and paste on poster board.

Making Friends cards

Directions: Copy on colored paper, laminate, and cut into cards.

Making Friends

Use a greeting.

Introduce yourself.

Talk about something you have in common.

QUEST Program II: Social Skills Curriculum for Middle School Students with Autism
© by JoEllen Cumpata and Susan Fell. Future Horizons, Inc.

It's the first day of school and you walk into homeroom.

You are in science class and your teacher assigns lab partners.

During an English class introduction another student mentions he likes dogs.

In foods class, both you and another student have trouble using the can opener.

In physical education you notice another student shooting baskets.

During social studies you hear a student talking about his trip to Japan.

In math your teacher mentions that one of his students needs a tutor.

You see two students looking at a video game catalog during lunch.

You hear an announcement for football team sign-up after school.

The daily announcements mention a chess club meeting.

Two students are showing each other pictures of their cats.

In computer class, your teacher announces you will be creating your own Web site.

In choir your teacher decides who sings soprano, alto, tenor, and bass.

In wood shop class another student notices your birdhouse and says he really likes it.

In drama class you sit in the back and notice another student does, too.

In art class, your teacher announces you will be working with clay.

QUEST Program II: Social Skills Curriculum for Middle School Students with Autism
© by JoEllen Cumpata and Susan Fell. Future Horizons, Inc.

QUEST Program II UPDATE!

Dear Parent,

This week your child has been working hard in QUEST Program II to master the skill of

Making and Keeping Friends

Together we have learned and practiced:

- Greeting new friends at school.

- Talking about things they have in common.

- Continuing friendships by doing things together at lunch and after school.

You can help your child practice at home by:

- Asking your child about students in his/her classes, e.g., "I know science is your favorite subject. Are there any students in your class who also like to learn about the planets?" or "That project you made in wood shop was very interesting. What did other students in the class build?"

- Encourage your child to continue relationship-building throughout the day, e.g., "Lunch is a great time to talk about your new video game." or "Maybe we should invite the kids you are working with in English over this weekend to finish your project."

Thanks for your help!

Making Plans with Friends – Experiential Story

Many students have friends at school. When we have friends at school it can make our day more interesting and fun. Sometimes students who are friends at school also like to spend time together after school and on weekends. Spending time together after school and on weekends can show someone that you like them and want to be good friends. Spending time together after school and on weekends can also be interesting and fun.

Students often want to spend more time with friends they have made at school. Often students enjoy spending time together after school, on weekends, and during school breaks. Students can do homework or school projects together, watch TV, play video games, ride bikes, or just have fun. When students spend time together outside of school they can learn more about each other and become better friends

When a student wants to spend time with a friend after school or on weekends, they need to:

- Ask the student if they would like to get together after school?
- Talk about what you might do together outside of school.
- Ask the friend for their phone number or e-mail address.
- Get your parents permission to have a friend visit.
- Call the friend to make arrangements.

Students can spend time together outside of school by:

- Watching TV and movies
- Playing computer games
- Playing board games
- Going places together
- Talking
- Participating in sports activities
- Reading books or looking at magazines

It is nice to spend time with a school friend after school or on weekends. It can be fun and interesting.

I will try to spend time with my school friends at school and make plans to spend time together outside of school. I will try to ask my friends for their telephone number so I can call them at home. I will try to remember to call my friends to make arrangements for fun after school or on weekends. This is one way I can show my friends that I enjoy their company.

QUEST Program II: Social Skills Curriculum for Middle School Students with Autism
© by JoEllen Cumpata and Susan Fell. Future Horizons, Inc.

Making Plans with Friends – Activity Sheet

Materials

- ❑ "Making Plans with Friends" experiential story
- ❑ Making Plans with Friends handout
- ❑ Pencils

Procedure

- ❑ Read "Making Plans with Friends" experiential story.
- ❑ Give Making Plans with Friends handout to each student.
- ❑ Complete My Friends chart on Making Plans with Friends handout individually, and Activities questions as a group.
- ❑ Ask students to think about and write their thoughts in the Next Steps portion of handout.
- ❑ Discuss.
- ❑ Provide incentives for students who follow through with their plans.

Making Plans with Friends

Think about students you know and fill out the chart below.

Class	Friends or students who might be good friends	What we have in common	Good times to talk
Homeroom			
1st Hour			
2nd Hour			
3rd Hour			
4th Hour			
5th Hour			
6th Hour			
7th Hour			

QUEST Program II: Social Skills Curriculum for Middle School Students with Autism
© by JoEllen Cumpata and Susan Fell. Future Horizons, Inc.

Activities

1. Think about the after-school activities available at your school and in your community. List three you think you might enjoy.

    _____

    _____

2. Think about things you like to do in your free time and list three things below.

    _____

    _____

3. Look back at the My Friends chart you completed. Think about who you would like to become better friends with. Look at the activities above and think about one thing you might enjoy doing together. Finish by reading your next steps below.

Next Steps

-   Talk with my parents about making plans with my friend.

-   Agree on a date/time.

-   Speak with a friend and see if they are interested in getting together.

-   Get their phone number.

-   Finalize plans.

Have fun!

QUEST Program II UPDATE!

Dear Parent,

This week your child has been working hard in QUEST Program II to master the skill of

Making Plans with Friends

Together we have learned:

- Interests students have in common with their peers.

- Appropriate social activities friends can enjoy outside of school.

- Steps students can use to make social arrangements with peers:

  1. Get parental permission.

  2. Talk with friend(s) to see if they want to get together.

  3. Decide on date, time, and activity.

  4. Follow up with a phone call.

You can help your child practice at home by:

- Encouraging your child to plan a social date with a peer.

- Assisting your child by:

  1. Helping your child decide who to invite and what they can enjoy together. Ask your child to see their Making Plans with Friends handout from QUEST Program II for ideas.

  2. Writing down information your child will need in order to make arrangements with their peer.

  3. Assisting your child while they use the telephone to make arrangements.

  4. Speaking with the peer's parent to confirm arrangements.

  5. Providing transportation and supervision when needed.

Thanks for your help!

QUEST Program II: Social Skills Curriculum for Middle School Students with Autism
© by JoEllen Cumpata and Susan Fell. Future Horizons, Inc.

Using the Telephone – Experiential Story

When students want to have fun with friends after school, on weekends, or during the summer, they usually need to make plans ahead of time. Students might make plans at school, but often they need to use the telephone to make sure everyone has all the information to get together and have fun.

Using the telephone is a quick way to get information and make arrangements. Students who want to call their friends to make plans for fun activities need to:

- Make sure their parents agree with the plans.

- Find the telephone number of the person they want to call.

- Know what they are going to say.

- Have a pencil and paper ready to write down plans.

Students need to talk with their parents to decide who they should invite, when they should get together, and what they can do together. Parents usually prefer that students ask permission to get together with friends and make plans ahead of time.

Most parents have rules for using the telephone. Parents usually prefer that students call at convenient times and don't talk too long on the phone. Convenient times are times when the family is not sleeping, eating a meal, or doing other important things.

The telephone is used by everyone who lives in a house and should be shared. Many parents prefer that students talk briefly on the phone. Usually plans can be made in about ten minutes or less. If a student wants to talk for a longer time on the phone, it is a good idea to ask their parents if it is okay to use the phone for a longer time.

Parents usually know that other students will be calling to talk about homework or make plans for getting together. Parents may get upset if students call too often, at the wrong time, or if they stay on the phone too long.

I can make arrangements with my friends on the telephone. I will try to remember to ask my parents about our telephone rules, and get permission before I make plans with my friends. Using the telephone is a useful and quick way to make sure my friends and I have all the information we need to get together and have fun.

Using the Telephone – Activity Sheet

Materials

- ❑ "Using the Telephone" experiential story for each student.
- ❑ Telephone Script handout for each student.
- ❑ Telephone Conversation Examples cards.
- ❑ Two telephones (they do not need to be functional).

Procedure

- ❑ Read the "Using the Telephone" experiential story aloud.
- ❑ Read the Telephone Script handout.
- ❑ Spread the Telephone Conversation Examples cards upside down.
- ❑ Ask students to choose one card and pick a partner.
- ❑ Ask partners to demonstrate telephone conversation using telephones.
- ❑ Discuss what students could do to improve and what they did well.
- ❑ Remind students to ask permission at home from parents before using the telephone.

Telephone Script

It is nice to use the telephone to call friends. You can call friends to get information or to make arrangements for fun. You can also call friends just because you enjoy talking with them.

Before calling anyone on the telephone:

Decide

- Who will I call?

- Why am I calling?

- Will I be talking for longer than ten minutes?

- Should I ask permission from my parents?

Prepare Supplies

- Phone number

- Paper

- Pencil

Use the appropriate telephone script on the next page as you practice making your call.

Telephone Conversation: examples cards

Directions: Copy on colored paper, laminate, and cut into cards.

Dial your number and wait for the person on the other end to answer.

If you get a person:

You:	Hello, this is _____. May I please speak with _____.
Person:	Yes. One moment.
You:	Thank you.
Friend:	Hi!
You:	How are you?
Friend:	Great.
You:	The reason I called is _____.

Dial your number and wait for the person on the other end to answer.

If your friend is not home:

You:	Hello, this is _____. May I please speak with _____.
Person:	I'm sorry, _____ is not home right now.
You:	Could you ask _____ to call me when he/she gets home?
Person:	Sure.
You:	My number is _____. Thank you.

Dial your number and wait for the person on the other end to answer.

If you get an answering machine:

Machine:	Leave your name and number after the beep. "BEEP"
You:	Hello, this is _____. I was calling to speak with _____. Please call me back at _____. Thank you.

QUEST Program II: Social Skills Curriculum for Middle School Students with Autism
© by JoEllen Cumpata and Susan Fell. Future Horizons, Inc.

You need to know what the math homework is.

You need to know when the science project is due.

You are wondering if your friend is going to the school dance.

You are wondering if your friend is going to the school play.

Your friend has been home sick. You are wondering how they are feeling.

Your friend missed half a day of school. You are wondering how they are feeling.

You want to ask your friend if he/she would like to see a movie on Saturday.

You want to ask your friend to come over after school tomorrow.

Your friend's grandmother is in the hospital. You want to see how she is doing.

You want to invite your friend to your birthday party.

You just saw a good movie and you want to tell your friend about it.

You are excited about a new video game you just got and want to tell your friend.

You want to ask your mom if your friend can come over for dinner.

You want to ask your dad if he will be home by 6:00 p.m. to take you and your friend to a movie.

QUEST Program II: Social Skills Curriculum for Middle School Students with Autism
© by JoEllen Cumpata and Susan Fell. Future Horizons, Inc.

Using the Telephone – Activity Sheet

Materials

- ❏ "Using the Telephone" experiential story for each student.

- ❏ Telephone Log handout for each student.

Procedure

- ❏ Read the "Using the Telephone" experiential story aloud.

- ❏ Hand out the Telephone Log.

- ❏ Explain to students that they will be expected to practice using the telephone at home.

- ❏ Ask students to log their telephone contacts and bring the log to school each week.

- ❏ Discuss contacts made and results.

My Telephone Log

Date	Person I Called	Phone Number	Result

QUEST Program II: Social Skills Curriculum for Middle School Students with Autism
© by JoEllen Cumpata and Susan Fell. Future Horizons, Inc.

QUEST Program II UPDATE!

Dear Parent,

This week your child has been working hard in QUEST Program II to master the skill of

Using the Telephone

Together we have learned:

- Why the telephone is important when making plans with friends.

- Telephone etiquette: when to call, how long to speak to friends.

- How to share information with friends on the telephone.

You can help your child practice at home by:

- Helping your child decide who they can call on the telephone and what information they will share.

- Suggesting your child use the telephone to gain information, e.g., "Why don't you give Katie a call to make sure she is coming with us to the mall tomorrow?" or "It is probably a good idea for you to call Billy to confirm your plans for the movies."

- Using the attached telephone scripts to help your child rehearse telephone conversations before and during calls.

Thanks for your help!

Modesty – Experiential Story

Students in middle and high school are growing quickly. Their bodies are changing because they are becoming teenagers and young adults. This is called puberty.

Becoming more like an adult is something most middle school students are happy about. It is normal for students to look at their own private body parts when they are in puberty. Private body parts are those parts that are covered when we wear bathing suits. Students can look at their private body parts at home, in their bedroom, or bathroom.

Middle school students do not show their private body parts to other students or adults. Students also do not touch other student's private body parts, or let anyone touch them, either. Showing private body parts in school makes students feel uncomfortable and embarrassed, and it is against school rules. Keeping your private body parts covered is called MODESTY.

At school during gym class, students get undressed in a locker room for class or to swim. When students get undressed in a locker room, they should not touch each other or stare at other student's body parts. It is okay to get ready for gym or swimming in a locker room at school.

Sometimes doctors or parents need to see private body parts. It is okay for doctors and parents to see student's body private body parts in a doctor's office or at home.

I will not touch my private body parts in class or in school except when I use the bathroom. I will keep my private parts covered at school except when I change for gym or swimming class. I will not let other students look at or touch my private body parts.

In middle school I will be modest about my private body parts. When I am modest I am comfortable and not embarrassed, and I am following school rules.

QUEST Program II: Social Skills Curriculum for Middle School Students with Autism
© by JoEllen Cumpata and Susan Fell. Future Horizons, Inc.

Modesty – Activity Sheet

Materials

- ❏ "Modesty" experiential story for each student
- ❏ Good Decision/Bad Decision cards
- ❏ Modesty scenario cards

Procedure

- ❏ Read "Modesty" experiential story.
- ❏ Explain that if students find themselves in a situation where they feel uncomfortable, it is important to make the right decision.
- ❏ Read one of the Modesty scenario cards aloud.
- ❏ Ask students what they would do if they were in this situation.
- ❏ Place Modesty scenario cards in the center of the table.
- ❏ Give each student a Good Decision and Bad Decision card.
- ❏ Ask student to choose and read a Modesty scenario card and tell group what they would do in this situation.
- ❏ Ask group members to hold up Good or Bad Decision cards to indicate if they feel the student made a good or bad decision.
- ❏ Discuss.

Good Decision/Bad Decision cards

Directions: Copy on colored paper. Use one color for Good Decision cards and another for Bad Decision cards. Laminate, and cut into cards.

Modesty scenario cards

Directions: Copy on colored paper, laminate, and cut into cards.

Good Decision

Bad Decision

Good Decision

Bad Decision

Good Decision

Bad Decision

Good Decision

Bad Decision

You are changing in the locker room for gym and a student takes your uniform shorts.

You are swimming in the pool and another student keeps trying to grab your swimsuit.

You are in the shower at school and students are looking at a chubby new student.

You are at the beach and a 3-year-old girl takes off her bathing suit top.

You are in the bathroom at school and two students keep watching you.

You are in the bathroom at the mall and a mother is changing her baby's diaper.

You accidentally walk in when someone is in the bathroom.

You see a student put his hands in his pants.

Someone touches your private parts.

A student tells you to go hug another student.

A student asks you to dance at a school dance.

A student asks you to give another student a kiss.

You see two students hugging at a school dance.

A nurse asks you to get undressed and put on a hospital gown so your doctor can examine you.

A student tells you that it is OK for middle school students to hug each other.

A student tells you to pull down another student's pants in the locker room.

QUEST Program II: Social Skills Curriculum for Middle School Students with Autism
© by JoEllen Cumpata and Susan Fell. Future Horizons, Inc.

QUEST Program II UPDATE!

Dear Parent,

This week your child has been working hard in QUEST Program II to master the skill of

Modesty

Together we have learned:

- Ways students exhibit modesty at school and in the community.

- Ways to recognize an inappropriate or uncomfortable situation.

- Effective assertiveness skills.

You can help your child practice at home by:

- Discussing your personal family values regarding modesty (expected dress and behavior both during and outside of school).

- Monitoring the TV, movies, video games, and Web sites your child has access to, and discussing any questionable or inappropriate behavior they observe, e.g., "The students in that movie were kissing in the hall at school. Do you think that is appropriate?" or "The teenagers in that video were dressed inappropriately. What would happen at school if they dressed like that? "

- Helping your child rehearse assertiveness skills, e.g., "What would you say if someone tried to hug you at school?" or "What could you do if another student wanted to look at an inappropriate Web site?"

Thanks for your help!

Recognizing and Dealing with Gossiping, Bullying and Teasing – Experiential Story

Most students want to be friendly. Unfortunately, some students can be mean from time to time. Students who are mean might have learned to act this way because someone else has hurt them. Mean students might also want to make friends, but not know how. Sometimes students say mean things because they haven't thought about how it might make someone else feel. Sometimes students just think it is funny.

Students might insult another student or tell stories about them that are not true. This is called gossip. Often gossip is not true, and stories become more complicated and destructive as people spread the rumors. If students hear someone gossiping they can try to change the subject or use a quick exit line, like "I don't really want to talk about this," and leave the uncomfortable conversation. It is OK to try to stop the gossip by saying, "He is my friend, and I don't think that is true. Let's talk about something else." If students hear mean things have been said about them, it is best to speak in private to the person spreading the gossip, and ask them to stop.

Some friends like to tease each other in a humorous way. Friends may laugh, give a gentle push, or call each other names, but usually friends who tease each other don't want to be hurtful. Friends may need to talk about how much teasing is OK.

Some students like to bully or tease others to be mean. Usually they will call another student a bad name, criticize them, or even threaten them. When students try to make someone feel bad or scared, they are not being friends. If students tease or bully another student, they can try to ignore it and walk away. Usually bullies will stop if no one pays attention to them. If students keep saying mean things, or if they threaten another student, it is best to tell an adult. This is against school rules, and adults will usually work with the mean student to correct his or her behavior.

Most students want to be friendly, but some tease or bully others. Some friends even tease each other and might need to talk about it if it gets out of hand. If a student teases or bullies, students can ignore them, use a quick exit line, or walk away. If teasing keeps happening, or if someone threatens a student, they should always tell an adult.

QUEST Program II: Social Skills Curriculum for Middle School Students with Autism
© by JoEllen Cumpata and Susan Fell. Future Horizons, Inc.

Recognizing and Dealing with Gossiping, Bullying and Teasing – Activity Sheet

Materials

- ❑ "Recognizing and Dealing with Gossiping, Bullying, and Teasing" experiential story
- ❑ You Have Choices poster
- ❑ Gossiping, Bullying, Teasing scenario cards

Procedure

- ❑ Read "Recognizing and Dealing with Gossiping, Bullying, and Teasing" experiential story.
- ❑ Display You Have Choices poster in the room; discuss the choices listed and times you might use each.
- ❑ Ask each student to select a Gossiping, Bullying, and Teasing scenario card.
- ❑ Ask students to read cards aloud one at a time.
- ❑ Discuss if situation on card is gossiping, bullying, or teasing.
- ❑ Discuss which strategy from You Have Choices poster would be most useful.

You Have Choices poster

Directions: Enlarge and paste on poster board.

Gossiping, Bullying, Teasing scenario cards

Directions: Copy on colored paper, laminate, and cut into cards.

You Have Choices!
Dealing with Gossiping, Bullying, and Teasing

Ignore it	Use a quick exit line	Use humor

Talk about it in a friendly way	Walk away	Get an adult

You drop the football in PE and your friend calls you "clumsy."

A student in the hall who you don't know says, "Hey idiot" to you.

You are playing a computer game and another student tells you to quit hogging the computer.

You spill your milk at lunch and someone at your table laughs.

A student on the playground pushes you down and says, "I'm going to kick your butt after school."

You see a group of kids on your way home from school and they point and laugh at you.

Outside during lunch, two boys run by you and say, "Hey nerd, wanna play basketball?"

Your two best friends find out you flunked your math test and call you a "loser."

Two girls in your science class tell you to move over to the other side of the room because they need to talk in private.

One of your friends is at your house and says, "Your house stinks!"

You walk by two students in the hall and as you look at them one says, "Mind your own business geek!"

One of your friends tells you they heard two kids saying you like to eat dirt.

You are throwing a ball around at lunch and two kids take the ball away.

Your best friend grabs your candy bar and throws it to another friend at your lunch table.

A student comes into your stall in the bathroom and tells you they are going to punch you on the bus.

You are at your friend's house and they e-mail another student with angry words and say the e-mail is from you.

Your friends come up with a nickname for you that you don't like.

You say hello to a student in the hall and they ignore you.

A boy in your English class keeps knocking your books off your desk when the teacher isn't looking.

A friend is at your house and wants to call another student and call them a loser.

QUEST Program II UPDATE!

Dear Parent,

This week your child has been working hard in QUEST Program II to master the skill of

Recognizing and Dealing with Gossiping, Teasing, and Bullying

Together we have learned:

- The difference between friendly teasing and mean teasing.

- How to use a "quick exit line" to leave an uncomfortable situation.

- Ways to respond assertively when another student has been mean.

You can help your child learn more at home by:

- Helping your child understand the difference between friendly roughhousing or teasing and dangerous aggression, and moving them toward the appropriate solution, e.g., "I've seen you, Tom, and Jack horsing around and calling each other names at home and having fun, but it sounds like you boys might be getting too rough sometimes. Maybe the three of you need to talk about setting some rules about name-calling and wrestling." or "I know you have been avoiding Chris lately because he pushed you down and that frightened you. I know he was angry, but he is your friend and I don't think he was trying to hurt you. Would it be a good idea if we talked it over with him?" or "I know you really like Stacey, but when a student tells you they are going to hurt another student after school, we need to let your principal know. We don't want anyone getting hurt."

Thanks for your help!

QUEST Program II: Social Skills Curriculum for Middle School Students with Autism
© by JoEllen Cumpata and Susan Fell. Future Horizons, Inc.

Resisting Peer Pressure – Experiential Story

Most students like to be friendly and spend time with other students. Students spend a lot of time together in school. Some students also like to get together after school and on weekends. Most students like to have friends. When friends are together they usually feel happy and comfortable.

Sometimes students think that they can have more friends if they act silly, make students laugh, or do everything other students ask them to do, even if these things are against school rules. Some students like to boss other students around by asking them to do things that make them feel uncomfortable or that are against school rules.

PEER PRESSURE is when a student does something they know is wrong because they want someone to like them. Students who do things that are against school rules, or who ask you to do things that are against school rules, are not good choices for friends. When you spend time with these students you may feel pressure to do things you know are wrong, or things that make you uncomfortable. Doing things you know are wrong to make other students laugh, or to please other students, is not a good way to make friends. Usually these things only get you into trouble.

Some students make fun of other students or say bad things about them. This is called GOSSIP. Some students take things that don't belong to them. This is THEFT. Some students push or hit other students. This is called ASSAULT. Some even drink alcohol or use illegal drugs outside of school. Some students think it is OK to say inappropriate things, look at or touch other students' private body parts. This is called HARASSMENT.

Gossip, theft, assault, drug use, and harassment are all against school rules and can make you feel uncomfortable. Students may also throw food in the lunchroom, look at inappropriate Web sites on the school computer, or say something disrespectful to a teacher. These things are also against the school rules. Even though some of these things may seem fun at first, they are all against school rules. Students who do things that are against school rules will need to go talk with the principal. They might get a detention or a suspension.

It is important for students to stop and think before they do something that might be against school rules. When students take the time to stop and think before they act, they might be able to make a better decision and stay out of trouble.

Students who feel uncomfortable because another student wants them to do something wrong should do three things:

1. Ignore the student
2. Walk away
3. Tell an adult if the student doesn't leave you alone.

I can stop and think before I do something I know is wrong. I can pick friends who follow the school rules. I will ignore students who ask me to do things that make me feel uncomfortable, or who ask me to do things I know are wrong. When I stop and think before I act, I can be a successful student.

Resisting Peer Pressure – Activity Sheet

Materials

- ❑ "Resisting Peer Pressure" experiential story for each student
- ❑ Sally and Sam's Decisions posters (one for girls, one for boys)
- ❑ Decision cards
- ❑ Good Decision/Bad Decision cards
- ❑ Sticky poster tack

Procedure

- ❑ Read "Resisting Peer Pressure" experiential story.
- ❑ Explain that if students find themselves in situations where they feel uncomfortable, it is important to make the right decision.
- ❑ Help students to understand what "uncomfortable" feelings are.
- ❑ Display the Sally and Sam's Decisions posters.
- ❑ Attach Decision Cards to poster with sticky poster tack.
- ❑ Give each student a Good Decision and Bad Decision card.
- ❑ Ask one student to choose a Decision Card from poster and read it aloud.
- ❑ Ask a student to tell the class what he/she would do in that situation.
- ❑ Ask the group to hold up a Good Decision or Bad Decision card to represent whether they felt the student made a good or bad decision.
- ❑ Discuss.

Sally and Sam's Solutions posters

Directions: Enlarge and paste on poster board.

Decision cards

Directions: Copy on colored paper. Cut and fold at dotted lines so situation is hidden. Attach to Sally's Decision poster with sticky poster tack.

QUEST Program II: Social Skills Curriculum for Middle School Students with Autism
© by JoEllen Cumpata and Susan Fell. Future Horizons, Inc.

Sally's Solutions
Open the cards and help Sally fight Peer Pressure!

A student comes up to Sally and asks her if they can copy her homework.

A student asks Sally to hide another student's calculator.

Sally sees two students smoking a cigarette after school and they ask her if she wants one.

Sally is waiting outside the principal's office. Another student tells her to go into the empty principal's office and get a pencil for him.

Sally is eating lunch and a student tells her she forgot her lunch money and asks her for a dollar.

Three students tell Sally to put a note in another student's locker.

QUEST Program II: Social Skills Curriculum for Middle School Students with Autism
© by JoEllen Cumpata and Susan Fell. Future Horizons, Inc.

Sam's Solutions
Open the cards and help Sam fight Peer Pressure!

Sam sees two students taking another student's clothes while he is in the shower.

Sam is standing with three students. They are saying that another student is really stupid because he fell on the playground.

Everyone is supposed to be paying attention to the teacher, but the student sitting next to Sam keeps telling a joke.

Sam lost his music for choir. Another student tells him he knows the teacher keeps extras in her desk.

Students playing with the school football tell Sam if he throws it over the fence they will give him $1.

Four students ask Sam to look at an inappropriate Web site at school.

QUEST Program II UPDATE!

Dear Parent,

This week your child has been working hard in QUEST Program II to master the skill of

Resisting Peer Pressure

Together we have learned:

- What a peer is, and what peer pressure means.

- Peer behaviors that are against school rules including gossip, stealing, assault, drug and alcohol use, and harassment.

- Ways to avoid involvement with students who are making bad choices.

You can help your child learn more at home by:

- Practicing ways your child can resist peer pressure, e.g., "What would you do if your best friend told you to stick a pack of gum in your pocket at the drugstore without paying for it?" or "How would you handle it if a student you really liked was saying bad things about one of your friends at lunch?"

- Watching TV shows or movies that illustrate peer interaction and discussing choices students have regarding peer issues.

Thanks for your help!

Participating in an After-School Activity – Experiential Story

Most middle schools and high schools offer clubs, sports teams, dances, and other activities after school. These activities are planned to encourage students to socialize with their current friends, meet new friends and have fun. Many students are excited and happy to attend these activities. Some students feel nervous, confused, uncomfortable, angry, or even bored when they attend these activities. All these feelings are OK.

When students feel uncomfortable about attending after-school activities, sometimes it is because they are not sure how to act around other students, or because they think they might do something that would make them feel embarrassed. Knowing the rules, and learning more about what to do at an activity can help students feel more comfortable.

Schools usually have certain rules students must follow at after-school activities. These rules are part of the school code of conduct. Students usually try to act friendly at these activities and fit in with the other students. Sometimes students do things at after-school activities that are unusual, mean, or silly. Friends might feel uncomfortable being around students who act unusual, mean, or silly. Friends like to spend time with other students who act appropriately at after-school activities.

When students want to go to an after-school activity, they should discuss it first with their parents. Parents need to know the date and time of the activity, and they may also need other information about the activity. If the activity costs money, students may need to ask their parents for money for a ticket.

After students have their parent's permission to attend an after-school activity, they will probably need to buy a ticket or sign up for the activity. Homeroom teachers announce activities; they are posted on signs around school; and they are usually heard on the morning announcements as well. Tickets are usually on sale at lunchtime in the hall by the cafeteria. Students usually need to stand in line and wait their turn when they buy a ticket.

It is OK to go to an after-school activity alone or with friends, but many students feel more comfortable if they attend with a friend. Students can talk to their friends or classmates to see who will be attending. One way to do this is to walk up to a group of friends, stand an arm's-length away, give a greeting, and ask, "Are you going to the All School Fun Night next week?" Students can decide to go together or to meet somewhere at the school before the activity.

Another way students can be more comfortable at an after-school activity is to take some time at the beginning of the activity to watch other students and see what they are doing. If most of the students are standing at a basketball game, it is probably OK to stand. If most of the students are dancing at a school party, it is OK to dance. Watching other students is one way to learn more about what behavior is expected at the activity. Behaving appropriately will help students feel comfortable and have fun.

Three ways students can behave appropriately at all after-school activities or clubs is to: wait their turn, keep their hands and feet to themselves, and use appropriate language. If a student sees other students behaving inappropriately, like being too loud or rough, they should walk away from those students.

Going to after-school activities is one way students can make and keep friends and have fun. Sometimes it takes time before students feel comfortable at after-school activities, but usually the more often students participate, the better they will feel. Talking with parents about after school activities, making plans to attend with friends, watching how other students act, and behaving appropriately, are all ways students can feel more comfortable and have fun at after school activities.

Participating in an After-School Activity – Activity Sheet

Materials

- ❑ "Participating in an After-School Activity" experiential story for each student
- ❑ School calendar of events

Procedure

- ❑ Read "Participating in an After-School Activity" experiential story.
- ❑ Provide each student with school calendar of events.
- ❑ Discuss activities available and decide as a group which activity the group will attend.
- ❑ Familiarize group with activity dress, setting, music, lighting, transportation, fee, refreshments, etc.
- ❑ Assign the activity as homework.
- ❑ E-mail or call parents to encourage support of participation in activity.
- ❑ QUEST Program II staff attend activity and monitor student behavior, concerns, and questions.
- ❑ Discuss after event.

QUEST Program II: Social Skills Curriculum for Middle School Students with Autism
© by JoEllen Cumpata and Susan Fell. Future Horizons, Inc.

QUEST Program II UPDATE!

Dear Parent,

This week your child has been working hard in QUEST Program II to master the skill of

Participating in an After-School Activity

Together we have learned:

- Why students attend after-school events with peers.

- How to decrease anxiety and worry before and during social events.

- Steps students can use to make social arrangements with peers:

    1. Get parental permission.

    2. Ask friend(s) if they want to get together.

    3. Decide on date, time, and activity.

    4. Follow up with a phone call.

You can help your child practice at home by:

- Encouraging your child to participate in after-school clubs, sports, or activities. Research indicates that social discomfort increases with isolation and decreases as children are exposed to safe social situations.

- Assisting your child by:

    1. Helping your child decide what activity or club would be most interesting or fun.

    2. Discussing the event or club with school staff if necessary.

    3. Providing your child with money for tickets, or supplies for a club.

    4. Encouraging your child to make plans with other peers who are attending the activity or club.

    5. Providing transportation and supervision when needed.

Thanks for your help!

Dating – Experiential Story

In middle or high school, sometimes a girl and a boy student who have been friends for a while start to feel that the other person is very special. Sometimes they decide they are going to date. Not all students date in middle school or high school, but some do. Dating is sometimes also called "going together," "being boyfriend and girlfriend," or "hanging out."

Most students talk with their parents to decide what the rules should be about socializing with friends. Some parents prefer that students wait until high school or even later to date. Some parents feel more comfortable if girls and boys socialize in a group. It is important that students talk with their parents about dating before they decide to "go together."

When students decide to date it is because they feel happy to be around each other, they have been friends for a while (usually at least a month), and they want other students to know that they are special friends.

Usually a boy asks a girl to be his girlfriend, but it is also OK for a girl to ask a boy to be her boyfriend. When a student wants to ask another student to date or "hang out" they usually wait until a private time when there are no other students around. They sometimes have lunch together, walk together in the halls or home from school. Students then ask, "Do you want to hang out after school?" or "Do you want to get together this weekend?" or "Do you want to go to the school party together?"

Sometimes a friend might not want to hang out together, so they may say, "No." This is OK. It just means that the girl or the boy will stay friends, but not date. It may also mean that the student's parents have a family rule about dating and do not allow it yet. While students are dating each other they usually also agree to say they are not dating any other student. Middle school students date only one student at a time.

When students date they sometimes:

- Call each other at home on the telephone
- E-mail or instant message each other
- Eat lunch together
- Spend time together outside of school
- Walk home from school together
- Spend time together at school parties or dances

If I have known someone for a long time I might think that they are a special friend. If I would like to spend more time with them, I should talk with my parents to see what their rules are about dating. If my parents approve, I can ask them to hang out after school or on weekends. I might even ask them to be my boyfriend or girlfriend. We can socialize outside of school, get to know each other better and have fun together.

QUEST Program II: Social Skills Curriculum for Middle School Students with Autism
© by JoEllen Cumpata and Susan Fell. Future Horizons, Inc.

Dating – Activity Sheet

Materials

- ❑ "Dating" experimental story
- ❑ Dating poster
- ❑ Dating cards
- ❑ Sticky poster tack
- ❑ Overhead markers
- ❑ Wipes

Procedure

- ❑ Read "Dating" experimental story
- ❑ Display Dating poster
- ❑ Lay Dating cards face down on the table
- ❑ Ask one student to choose a Dating card and fasten it with sticky poster tack to the top box on the Dating poster
- ❑ Ask students to volunteer to continue the conversation by writing in the conversation bubbles on the poster
- ❑ Discuss possible responses

Dating poster

Directions: Enlarge, paste on poster board, and laminate.

Dating cards

Directions: Copy on colored paper, laminate, and cut into cards.

What would you say if ...

QUEST Program II: Social Skills Curriculum for Middle School Students with Autism
© by JoEllen Cumpata and Susan Fell. Future Horizons, Inc.

You want to go to the school dance with someone you have been friends with for a long time.

You think it would be fun to go to a movie this weekend with someone you really like.

You want to get a group of kids together to go bowling.

Your parent has told you that you can ask two students to join your family on a weekend camping trip.

Your mother told you that you can invite both boy and girl students over for your party.

Tomorrow is a half-day of school, and you think it might be fun to go out to lunch with a special friend.

Your grade is planning a Cedar Point trip and you would like to hang out with friends during the trip.

You are at a school dance and you see someone you would like to dance with across the room.

Your father told you that you could invite a friend to go swimming at the park.

Your grandfather invited you to go fishing and told you to bring a friend.

You bought a new video game and thought it would be fun to show it to a few friends.

Your parent told you that you could have a sleepover.

QUEST Program II: Social Skills Curriculum for Middle School Students with Autism
© by JoEllen Cumpata and Susan Fell. Future Horizons, Inc.

The school is having a fun night and you thought you might go with a few friends.

You just got a new puppy and you would like to show it to a few friends.

You would like to ask someone you really like to go to the prom.

Your aunt got you tickets to a concert and you would like to ask someone you really like.

QUEST Program II UPDATE!

Dear Parent,

This week your child has been working hard in QUEST Program II to master the skill of

Dating

Together we have learned:

- How to arrange a social event with friends.

- The importance of discussing arrangements first with parents.

- Appropriate middle school peer socialization practices.

You can help your child learn more at home by:

- Discussing your personal family values regarding socializing and dating.

- Encouraging family discussion and questions regarding adolescent social relationships, e.g., "When middle school students get together after school, what do they like to do?" or "Mrs. Smith told me her son is going on a date. How old do you think students should be before they date?"

- Preparing your child for school dances and social events by discussing possible student interactions, e.g., "If you see your friend tonight at the dance, how could you ask her/him to dance?" or "If another student asked you to go to a movie and you didn't want to go what could you say? "

Thanks for your help!

QUEST Program II Unit Four - Making Friends and Interacting with Peers Unit Evaluation

Student Name _____ Date _____

Evaluator _____

We have just completed a unit in QUEST Program II on Making Friends and Interacting with Peers. Please fill out the rating scale below to assist us in determining how well your student has generalized the skills taught, and if you have noticed improvement in their level of skill over the past six weeks. Check all boxes that apply below.

O=Often S=Sometimes N=Never I=Improvement   **How Often Skill Is Observed**

Skill	O	S	N	I
Appreciate the value of friendship Identify children who might be good choices for friends. Share information about other students.				
Understand and demonstrate ways to initiate friendships Use greetings with new friends, discuss topics of interest, and things in common. Approach new friends without direction from adults.				
Attempt socialization outside of the school setting Discuss weekend, evening, or after-school opportunities for friendship building. Agree to socialize after school hours. Solicit other students to make arrangements for socialization outside of school.				
Make telephone arrangements with friends Use the telephone to discuss time, date, and location of social activities with friends. Leave messages appropriately.				
Appreciate and demonstrate appropriate modesty when around peers and adults Refrain from exposing or touching private body parts in public. Exhibit comfort level using public restrooms or changing facilities. Refrain from gazing at or touching others using public facilities.				
Understand the difference between friendly teasing, humor, gossip, and threats Tolerate and manage friendly teasing with humor, or assertive statements. Report threats or mean teasing to helpful adults.				

O-Often S=Sometimes N=Never I=Improvement   **How Often Skill Is Observed**

Skill	O	S	N	I
Understand and practice assertiveness skills with peers Report uncomfortable peer situations to adults. Use assertive refusal statements with peers regarding social activities, rules, and risky behavior.				
Appreciate and attempt to participate in after-school activities List and identify at least one after-school activity they might enjoy. Make appropriate arrangements regarding permission slips, transportation, and fees. Attempt participation.				
Understand and comfortably discuss the concept of dating Discuss school social event behaviors like dancing, hugging, hand-holding, etc., with trusted adults. Role-play responses to the assertive social behaviors of peers. Act appropriately in peer social situations, dances, parties, or group social activities.				

Comments_____

_____

Thank you for your input!

Unit 5

Personal Safety

Goal

To increase student awareness of personal safety, and practice skills needed for safety at home and in the community

Objectives

- To learn basic home-safety rules and have easy access to important safety information when home alone.

- To understand how and when to use the telephone, including the use of 911 during a home emergency.

- To react appropriately when smoke or fire alarms sound, or if fire is spotted in the home.

- To know the proper steps to take to ensure personal safety when separated from a group in a public place.

- To learn and appreciate the necessity for utilizing personal safeguards when using the computer.

- To recognize the possible dangers involved when driving with peers and use appropriate safeguards.

- To gain a basic understanding of popular illegal substances used by peers and practice refusal strategies.

QUEST Program II: Social Skills Curriculum for Middle School Students with Autism
© by JoEllen Cumpata and Susan Fell. Future Horizons, Inc.

Experiential Stories, Activities and Parent Updates

Stories can be read by parents, teachers, or students. Often students gain a deeper understanding of skills when stories can be discussed in detail in a group setting. Asking students to summarize paragraphs, relate their personal experiences, and complete activities are all effective ways to increase generalization of skills. Parent Updates provide additional ways to continue learning at home. The letter "A" denotes advanced sections appropriate for students in their second or third year of the program.

Topics included in this unit are:

1. Being Home Alone

2. Using the Telephone in an Emergency

3. Smoke and Fire Alarm Safety

4. Being Separated from My Group

5. Internet and E-mail Safety - A

6. Driving with Others - A

7. Drugs, Alcohol, and Dangerous Behavior - A

Being Home Alone – Experiential Story

When students get older they start to become responsible for themselves. Middle or high school students might choose and purchase their own clothes, make their own snacks, schedule their own hair and medical appointments, stay home alone, or even care for other family members or relatives for a short time when their parents are out or at work. Not all parents allow their students to stay home alone, but some do. Being home alone is one way middle school students can begin to be responsible for caring for themselves.

Sometimes students who are home alone might watch TV or play a computer game, read a book or do some homework, make a snack or listen to music. It can be peaceful and comfortable to be home alone.

When students are home alone they are responsible for their own safety, so it is important to learn and remember home-safety rules. Parents usually have some safety rules that they think are very important. It is a good idea for middle school students to talk with their parents about their home-safety rules.

Parents usually have rules about using the telephone, the stove or other home appliances, having friends or other people over and knowing what to do in an emergency. Families can talk about important information, and share telephone numbers they can use to stay safe.

One way middle school students can remember home-safety rules and important telephone numbers is to have a Home-Safety Checklist on their refrigerator. Home-Safety Checklists help parents and students remember important information, telephone numbers and ways to be safe.

I can relax and have fun when I am home alone when I learn and remember home-safety rules. I can talk with my parents about home-safety. I can write down important information and telephone numbers on a Home-Safety Checklist and place it on my refrigerator at home. I will try to use a Home-Safety Checklist when I am home alone.

QUEST Program II: Social Skills Curriculum for Middle School Students with Autism
© by JoEllen Cumpata and Susan Fell. Future Horizons, Inc.

Being Home Alone – Activity Sheet

Materials

- ❑ "Being Home Alone" experiential story
- ❑ Student/Parent Home-Safety Questionnaire handouts
- ❑ Home-Safety Checklist handouts
- ❑ Pencils

Procedure

- ❑ Read "Being Home Alone" experiential story.
- ❑ Pass out Student/Parent Home Safety Questionnaire handout.
- ❑ Discuss questions on Student/Parent Home-Safety Questionnaire handout.
- ❑ Show students Home-Safety Checklist handouts and explain that each student will have the opportunity to create and laminate one for use at home after they and their parents provide safety information.
- ❑ Ask students to take Student/Parent Home-Safety Questionnaire handout home, discuss and complete with their parents.
- ❑ Explain the importance of family discussion regarding safety topics with the students.

IMPORTANT NOTE: Do not allow students to complete Student/Parent Home-Safety Questionnaire independently. This activity is meant to increase discussion at home regarding safety issues.

Student/Parent Home-Safety Questionnaire

QUEST Program II students are discussing personal safety and will be creating a Home-Safety Checklist in class.

Think about times your child might be home alone, or times you may be unavailable at home. Please discuss each area with your child and circle "YES" or "NO" below. List any special rules on the line under each statement.

When I am home alone am I allowed to ...

Answer the telephone   Yes   No

_____

Call people on the telephone   Yes   No

_____

Use the computer   Yes   No

_____

Use the internet   Yes   No

_____

Watch TV   Yes   No

_____

Read a book or do homework   Yes   No

_____

Listen to music   Yes   No

_____

Answer the door   Yes   No

_____

Leave the house   Yes   No

_____

Play in the yard   Yes   No

_____

Have a friend over   Yes   No

_____

Prepare food   Yes   No

_____

Please list people your child can call in case of an emergency.

Name _____   Phone _____

Name _____   Phone _____

Name _____   Phone _____

Please list any additional safety information or rules you feel are important in your home.

_____

_____

_____

_____

_____

Being Home Alone – Activity Sheet

Materials

- ❑ "Being Home Alone" experiential story
- ❑ Completed Student/Parent Home-Safety Questionnaire handouts
- ❑ Home-Safety Checklist handouts
- ❑ Pencils

Procedure

- ❑ Read "Being Home Alone" experiential story.
- ❑ Hand out Home-Safety Checklist.
- ❑ Ask students to use their completed Student/Parent Home-Safety Questionnaire handout to fill in spaces on Home-Safety Checklist.
- ❑ Discuss appropriate places to display the Home-Safety Checklist at home (typically on the refrigerator).
- ❑ Laminate Home-Safety Checklist and send home with students.

QUEST Program II: Social Skills Curriculum for Middle School Students with Autism
© by JoEllen Cumpata and Susan Fell. Future Horizons, Inc.

Home-Safety Checklist

My address is: _____

Important telephone numbers:

Police/fire: 911
_____

_____

_____

I need to follow these safety rules when I am home alone:

1. _____

2. _____

3. _____

4. _____

QUEST Program II UPDATE!

Dear Parent,

This week your child has been working hard in QUEST Program II to master the skill of

Being Home Alone

Together we have learned:

- Some middle school students are home alone from time to time.

- Parents have different rules about being home alone.

- A Home-Safety Checklist is one way to remember home safety rules.

You can help your child learn more at home by:

- Completing the Home-Safety Questionnaire with your child.

- Encouraging family discussion and questions regarding home safety, e.g., "If I was in the shower and someone you did not know came to the door, what would you do?" or "If you were home alone and you broke a lamp, what would you do?" or "If we were home together and I were to fall and hurt myself, who could you call?" or "Show me how you prepare a snack when you are home alone."

Thanks for your help!

QUEST Program II: Social Skills Curriculum for Middle School Students with Autism
© by JoEllen Cumpata and Susan Fell. Future Horizons, Inc.

Using the Telephone in an Emergency – Experiential Story

When students are home alone it is important that they know how to get help in case there is an emergency. Home emergencies don't happen very often but if they do, it is best to be prepared. Home emergencies include medical emergencies, like someone getting hurt or swallowing something dangerous; physical emergencies, like a fire or broken window; and personal emergencies, like receiving an unusual phone call, or a concern about a stranger near the home.

One way students can get help when they are home alone is by using the telephone. Students can call family members or friends who are listed on their Home-Safety Checklist when there is an emergency. Students can also dial 911.

It is important to remember that calling 911 is only appropriate during an emergency! Some things that happen when adults are gone are problems but not emergencies. If the problem can wait to be fixed until a parent gets home, students should not call 911. Problems that can wait might include a stopped-up toilet, a burnt-out light bulb, or even a pet throwing up in the living room.

Students can ask themselves three questions when there is a problem to decide if they should call 911:

1. Am I or another person in immediate danger?
2. Could I or another person be in danger if someone doesn't help?
3. Should I leave my home now?

If the student answers "yes" to any of these questions they should go to a safe place and call 911. If there is something dangerous in their home like a fire, a student should always go to a neighbor's house or another safe place and then call 911.

Dialing 911 will connect students with their local police or fire department. Trained emergency professionals are ready to help people who call 911. Sometimes they will give information on the phone, and sometimes they will send police, fire, or other emergency professionals to the home to handle the emergency.

When students call 911 they will be asked several questions. It is important that students stay calm so they can give accurate information. One way students can stay calm is to breathe deeply in their nose and out their mouth before they talk. The 911 emergency professional may ask them their name, age, and address. The professional may also ask other questions about the emergency situation.

I can decide if a problem is an emergency at home by asking myself if I or someone else is in danger. I can be calm during a home emergency by doing deep breathing and calling 911. I can give information to the emergency professional on the phone and get help. I will remember not to call 911 if the problem can wait until my parent gets home. When I follow these steps I will be safe at home.

Using the Telephone in an Emergency – Activity Sheet

Materials

- ❑ "Using the Telephone in an Emergency" experiential story
- ❑ To Dial or Not to Dial handouts
- ❑ Pencils

Procedure

- ❑ Read "Using the Telephone in an Emergency" experiential story.
- ❑ Hand out To Dial or Not to Dial handouts.
- ❑ Ask students to silently complete handout by circling "CALL" or "DON'T CALL" for each item.
- ❑ Read questions aloud one at a time.
- ❑ Ask students to discuss if they feel it would be appropriate to call 911 in each case.

QUEST Program II: Social Skills Curriculum for Middle School Students with Autism
© by JoEllen Cumpata and Susan Fell. Future Horizons, Inc.

To Dial or Not to Dial

(that is the question)

Sometimes when middle school students are at home they might experience a problem or home emergency. Look at the situations below, talk about what you would do, and circle the correct answer.

1.	Boys are playing baseball across the street and the ball breaks your front window.	CALL	DON'T CALL
2.	Your dog runs down the street.	CALL	DON'T CALL
3.	Your 3-year-old sister eats a marble.	CALL	DON'T CALL
4.	You are making some toast and you see flames coming out of the toaster.	CALL	DON'T CALL
5.	You smell something strong that makes you feel dizzy.	CALL	DON'T CALL
6.	You find your grandmother lying on the floor. She seems unconscious.	CALL	DON'T CALL
7.	You see a strange man in your backyard.	CALL	DON'T CALL
8.	Your father cuts his finger on a can lid.	CALL	DON'T CALL
9.	You are sitting reading and the light burns out.	CALL	DON'T CALL
10.	Your little brother falls down the stairs and says he can't move his leg.	CALL	DON'T CALL
11.	You turn on the TV and it doesn't work.	CALL	DON'T CALL
12.	You are watching TV and a news report interrupts your program telling you that there is a severe weather warning in your area.	CALL	DON'T CALL
13.	You hear your cat meowing from the roof.	CALL	DON'T CALL
14.	Your mother has not come home from work. She is 1 ½ hours late.	CALL	DON'T CALL

QUEST Program II UPDATE!

Dear Parent,

This week your child has been working hard in QUEST Program II to master the skill of

Using the Telephone in an Emergency.

Together we have learned:

- Three types of home emergencies.

- When it is appropriate to call 911.

- The importance of leaving the home before calling 911 in certain circumstances.

You can help your child learn more at home by:

- Reviewing the Home-Safety Checklist with your child (copy attached).

- Posting the Home-Safety Checklist in a easily visible area.

- Discussing possible emergency situations that could occur in your home and practicing safety responses, e.g., "If I was out and you saw sparks coming from the telephone pole in our yard, what would you do?" or "When do you think you should call 911?" or "If a small fire started in our toaster, what would you do?"or "When you are home alone with your younger brother/sister, what would you do if they swallowed a small toy?"

Thanks for your help!

QUEST Program II: Social Skills Curriculum for Middle School Students with Autism
© by JoEllen Cumpata and Susan Fell. Future Horizons, Inc.

Smoke and Fire Alarm Safety – Experiential Story

At school students practice fire drills. Fire drills prepare the students, teachers, and other people who work in school in case there is a fire. At home, fire safety is also important. It is helpful if students talk with their parents and families about ways to be prepared and safe at home in case there is a fire.

One way families can be safe is by installing and understanding smoke and fire alarms. Most homes, schools, and businesses have smoke detectors or smoke and fire alarm systems. These devices are designed to let people know when there is a danger of smoke or fire in a building. Usually smoke detectors can tell when smoke is in a room, and make a very loud noise to alert people in the building. This noise is designed to be annoying, and wake sleeping people or alert people in other rooms.

When families hear the smoke and fire alarm it is important that they know how to react. This usually means finding the source of the smoke and deciding if they need to leave their home to call 911, or if they can handle the smoke situation on their own. Sometimes, smoke detectors will sound when people are cooking on a stove, when their battery is low, or even when a bug gets into the smoke detector.

If students are home alone and their smoke and fire alarm sounds, it is best for them to leave the house and call 911 from another location. Emergency response professionals, such as firefighters, will respond to the fire. These professionals are trained to keep people and pets safe, put out the fire, and take care of the home.

Students and their families can also be safe if they talk about what to do if the smoke and fire alarm sounds when the family is home. Families can develop a Fire-Safety Plan to follow in case of smoke or fire. It is useful for the family to decide where to meet inside and outside of the home if there is a fire. When families decide on a safe meeting place they can make sure quickly that all family members are safe.

I can practice fire drills at school when the fire alarm sounds. I can talk with my family about fire safety and develop a Fire-Safety Plan. When I am alone, if the smoke detector makes a loud noise I can leave my home and call 911 from a neighbor's house. My family and I can be safe when we use smoke detectors, develop a Fire-Safety Plan, and talk about what to do if there is a fire in our home.

Smoke and Fire Alarm Safety – Activity Sheet

Materials

- ❏ "Smoke and Fire Alarm Safety" experiential story
- ❏ Home Design Items packets

Procedure

- ❏ Read "Smoke and Fire Alarm Safety" experiential story.
- ❏ Divide students into groups.
- ❏ Give each group a Home Design Items packet. It is helpful to create packets using different colored paper so groups do not argue regarding items.
- ❏ Ask students to design a home with a kitchen, living room, family room, two bathrooms and two bedrooms using items. Straight pieces are to be used as walls.
- ❏ Ask each group to use the pictures of the people, animals, or, fireman in the packet to devise safe exit routes from each room.
- ❏ Ask groups to demonstrate exit routes for the class.
- ❏ Discuss.

Home Design Items

Directions: Copy on colored paper, laminate, and cut. Create several sets for classroom groups. Place each set in a large envelope.

QUEST Program II: Social Skills Curriculum for Middle School Students with Autism
© by JoEllen Cumpata and Susan Fell. Future Horizons, Inc.

Chairs

Lamps

Tables

Sofas

 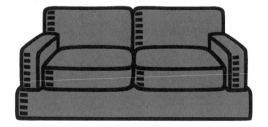

QUEST Program II: Social Skills Curriculum for Middle School Students with Autism
© by JoEllen Cumpata and Susan Fell. Future Horizons, Inc.

Beds

Toilets and Sinks

Appliances, Cabinets

Rugs

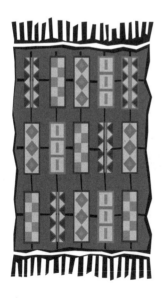  

Windows

Doors

Family Members, Pets & Firemen

QUEST Program II: Social Skills Curriculum for Middle School Students with Autism
© by JoEllen Cumpata and Susan Fell. Future Horizons, Inc.

Walls

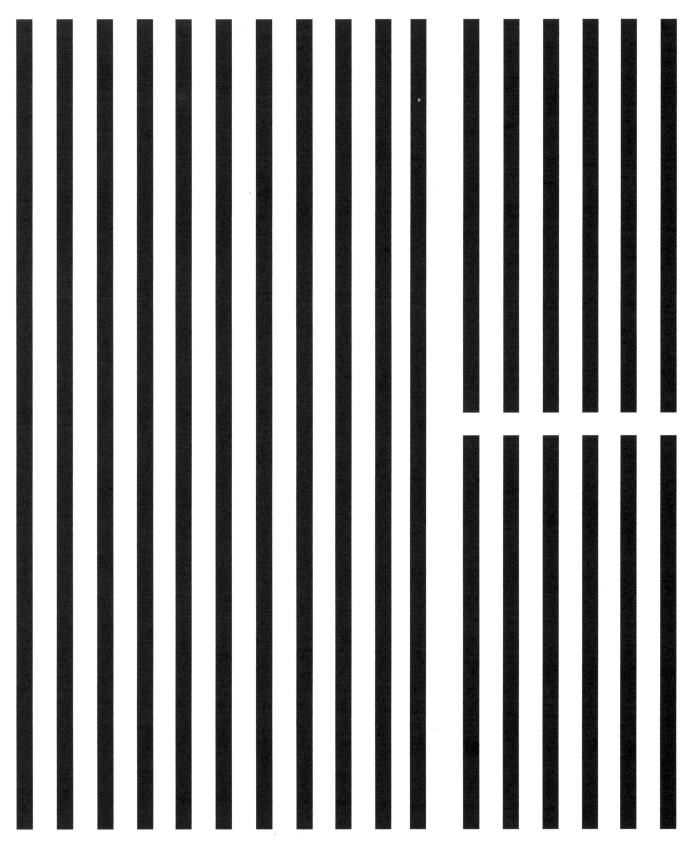

Smoke and Fire Alarm Safety – Activity Sheet

Materials

- ❏ "Smoke and Fire Alarm Safety" experiential story
- ❏ Family Fire Safety Plan handout

Procedure

- ❏ Read "Smoke and Fire Alarm Safety" experiential story.
- ❏ Ask students to take home Family Fire-Safety Plan handout and complete with their family.

QUEST Program II: Social Skills Curriculum for Middle School Students with Autism
© by JoEllen Cumpata and Susan Fell. Future Horizons, Inc.

Family Fire-Safety Plan

We have _____ smoke detectors in our home.

Our smoke detectors are located in

_____

_____

If there is a fire and we need to leave the house, this is where my family will meet to make sure we are all safe.

_____

If there is no adult at home and my smoke detector alarm goes off, I can go to _____'s house to get help or call 911.

If there is a small fire or smoke in my home, my parents want me to

_____

Draw your home fire escape route on the next page.

Family Fire-Safety Plan

This is how we can get out of the house in case of fire

This is where my family will meet if we need to
leave the house because of a fire

If there is no adult to home and the smoke detector goes off,
I can go here to call 911

QUEST Program II UPDATE!

Dear Parent,

This week your child has been working hard in QUEST Program II to master the skill of

Fire and Smoke Alarm Safety

Together we have learned:

- How fire and smoke alarms are used.

- What to do if a fire or smoke alarm goes off at home.

- How to complete a Family Fire-Safety Plan.

You can help your child learn more at home by:

- Completing the Family Fire-Safety Plan (attached) with your child.

- Discussing safe ways to react in a fire or smoke-related emergency, e.g., "Let me show you where our fire extinguisher is and how to use it."or "What would you do if you were home alone and our smoke/fire alarm went off?" or "If a small fire started on the stove, what would you do?" or "Where could you go to call 911 if our smoke/fire alarm went off?"

Thanks for your help!

Being Separated from My Group – Experiential Story

Students often visit public places with their class, other students, or with their families. Sometimes students are on a field trip or family outing. Sometimes students are visiting a public place to buy clothing, toys, or food items. Places students go might be inside a building, like a shopping mall, grocery store, museum, or movie theater. Students also might go to public places that are outside, like parks, camping facilities, and recreation areas.

When they are on an outing, students might become separated from their group. This could happen if a student becomes very interested in something or if they don't hear a direction given to the group. When this happens it is normal to feel frightened or anxious. One way to feel better and become rejoined with your group is to know what to do in this situation.

Before students visit a public place with their families, friends, or on a school trip, it is helpful to talk about what to do if anyone is separated from the group. Students who are separated from their group in a public place should use their cell phone to call their parent, a family member, or friend. But if students don't have a phone, they should do three things to help them become rejoined with their group:

1. **Stay in the same place for five to ten minutes** – Usually people from the group will come looking for a student as soon as they notice that he or she is missing.

2. **Find a helpful person** – When students are inside a building, helpful people are often employees who work in the building. They might be working a cash register, taking admission tickets, or sitting behind a desk. When students are outside, helpful people are usually in an office or building in the park or recreational area. Sometimes helpful people wear uniforms, like policemen, camp rangers, or store security personnel.

3. **Let the helpful person know you are separated from your group** – Helpful people will usually have some way of finding a group of people. Sometimes they will use a loudspeaker or telephone to find a student's group.

I will talk about what to do if I am separated from my group BEFORE I go on an outing with family, friends, or peers. If I am separated I can stay in the same place for five to ten minutes, find a helpful person, and let that person know that I have been separated from my group. Talking about and preparing a plan for what to do if I am separated from my group can make me feel comfortable on school trips, family outings, or when I'm out with my friends.

Being Separated from My Group – Activity Sheet

Materials

- ❑ "Being Separated from My Group" experiential story
- ❑ Help, I'm Lost! handout
- ❑ Being Separated from My Group scenario cards

Procedure

- ❑ Read "Being Separated from My Group" experiential story.
- ❑ Give each student a Help, I'm Lost! handout and review steps to follow if separated from a group.
- ❑ Ask a student to select a Being Separated from My Group scenario card and read aloud.
- ❑ Ask the student to decide what they would do in the situation.
- ❑ Discuss

Being Separated from My Group scenario cards

Directions: Copy on colored paper, laminate, and cut into cards.

Help, I'm Lost!
If you are lost, remember:

- Stay in the same spot for five to ten minutes.

- Call your parent, a family member, or friend if you have a cell phone.

- Find a helpful person. A store employee, security guard, or someone working at a cash register.

- Let the helpful person know you have been separated from your group.

QUEST Program II: Social Skills Curriculum for Middle School Students with Autism
© by JoEllen Cumpata and Susan Fell. Future Horizons, Inc.

What Do You Do?

You are at the zoo on a school field trip. You are looking at the monkeys when you notice that the group you were with is gone.

What Do You Do?

You are at the mall with your family shopping for school clothes. You are in the Disney store playing with a stuffed animal and you notice your family is not there.

What Do You Do?

You are outside at your city park celebrating your cousin's birthday. You were swinging on the swings and when you went back to the picnic area, your family was not there.

What Do You Do?

You are at the museum on a school field trip. You are looking at a display when you notice that the group you were with is gone.

What Do You Do?

You are at the grocery store with your mother. You stop to look at all the ice cream flavors and when you look up she is gone.

What Do You Do?

You are visiting relatives in Chicago. You and your family are window-shopping downtown. You notice an interesting window display. After a few moments, you go to join your family and cannot find them.

What Do You Do?

You are at the high school for a school play. You use the bathroom and when you come out your group is gone.

What Do You Do?

You are at a parade with your family and you notice a man selling balloons. You run after him and then notice your family is gone.

What Do You Do?

You are running track with the school team through the neighborhood and you stop to tie your shoes. When you look up, the team is gone.

What Do You Do?

You are at the airport with your family waiting to meet your aunt and uncle who are visiting from Florida. You are watching several people riding past on a small cart. When you turn around your family is gone.

What Do You Do?

You are riding your bike around the neighborhood and you see a stray dog. You follow him on your bike for several minutes when you finally realize you don't recognize the street.

What Do You Do?

You are at the movies with your friends. You are in line to buy popcorn when you notice your friends are gone.

QUEST Program II: Social Skills Curriculum for Middle School Students with Autism
© by JoEllen Cumpata and Susan Fell. Future Horizons, Inc.

QUEST Program II UPDATE!

Dear Parent,

This week your child has been working hard in QUEST Program II learning about personal safety and

Being Separated from My Group

Together we have learned:

- Three steps to follow if separated from a group

- Who "helpful people" are in cities, shops, museums, parks, and recreational areas

- How to approach a "helpful person" to get assistance.

You can help your child learn more at home by:

- Discussing the safety strategies below with your child before school field trips or family outings:

  1. **Use your cell phone to call a parent or family member.**

  2. **Stay in the same place for five to ten minutes** – Usually people from the group will come looking for a student as soon as they notice that he or she is missing.

  3. **Find a helpful person** – When students are inside a building, helpful people are often employees who work in the building. They might be working a cash register, taking admission tickets, or sitting behind a desk. When students are outside, helpful people are usually in an office, or building in the park, or recreational area. Sometimes helpful people wear uniforms, like policemen, camp rangers, or store security personnel.

  4. **Let the helpful person know you are separated from your group** – Helpful people will usually have some way of finding a group of people. Sometimes they will use a loudspeaker or telephone to find a student's group.

Thanks for your help!

Internet and E-mail Safety – Experiential Story

Middle and high school students are sometimes permitted to use the Internet or e-mail at school or at home. Searching for information on the Internet can be fun and interesting. Some students communicate with family and friends using e-mail or instant social media sites.

Once in a while, students may hear about or find a website or e-mail address that may be dangerous or inappropriate. Dangerous websites might show pictures of weapons or other types of violent objects or acts. Inappropriate websites might show pictures of people with few or no clothes on, or they might discuss racially or religiously discriminatory topics.

Sometimes when using the Internet or e-mail, students might be asked to type in their name, age, social security number, birth date, school, address or information about family or friends. This type of information is called "personal information." Giving personal information over the Internet, through e-mail or social media can be dangerous.

Students who e-mail each other or use social media might use abbreviations or codes that mean different things. Sometimes students type inappropriate or mean things into e-mails. Students need to remember that typing information or messages in a computer is like talking; however, the conversation is occurring via a computer instead. It is important to only use appropriate language and abbreviations. If students see inappropriate or mean messages on their e-mail or on a social media site, they should show this to their parents or another trusted adult. Students should never type inappropriate or mean messages to others.

It is important that students follow safety rules when they use the computer. Parents and students should talk about these rules together, because different families have different rules. To be safe on the computer, it is important not to type in personal information unless you have your parent's permission. If students hear about or accidentally find a dangerous or inappropriate website on the computer, they should exit out and talk about it with their parents.

When I remember computer safety rules, I can have fun, talk with friends, and find interesting information on the Internet, through e-mail and on social media sites. I can be safe on the Internet when I exit out of dangerous or inappropriate sites and when I don't give out any personal information. I can be careful not to e-mail inappropriate or mean words to other students. I can talk with my parents or teachers when I have a question or concern about computer safety.

QUEST Program II: Social Skills Curriculum for Middle School Students with Autism
© by JoEllen Cumpata and Susan Fell. Future Horizons, Inc.

Internet and E-mail Safety – Activity Sheet

Materials

- ❑ *Internet and E-Mail Safety* experiential story
- ❑ Internet and E-Mail Safety handout

Procedure

- ❑ Read *Internet and E-Mail Safety* experiential story.
- ❑ Give each student an Internet and E-Mail Safety handout.
- ❑ Ask them to read each situation and decide if the student in the situation was acting safely or unsafely while on the computer.
- ❑ Discuss.

Internet and E-mail Safety

Students do many things on the computer. Sometimes students can provide too much personal information and put themselves in danger. Students may also find an inappropriate site, or use inappropriate language while on the computer.

Read each situation below and decide if the student was "SAFE" or "UNSAFE." Circle your answer. Be ready to discuss your choice.

1. Jonah was taking a sports survey he found on the Internet and entered his date of birth, school, and name.

   ❑ SAFE   ❑ UNSAFE

2. Sara enjoys using social media and likes to add pictures of herself, her friends, and family.

   ❑ SAFE   ❑ UNSAFE

3. Bill likes to chat with friends while he does his homework. He sometimes talks to people online even if he doesn't recognize their screen name.

   ❑ SAFE   ❑ UNSAFE

4. John likes to purchase music on the computer. His parents have an account and let him type in their password and buy and download music when he asks their permission.

   ❑ SAFE   ❑ UNSAFE

5. Patty e-mails friends at school a lot. Sometimes friends say inappropriate things to Patty in e-mails, but she just sends nasty and inappropriate e-mails back to them.

   ❑ SAFE   ❑ UNSAFE

QUEST Program II: Social Skills Curriculum for Middle School Students with Autism
© by JoEllen Cumpata and Susan Fell. Future Horizons, Inc.

6. Patrick is working on a school project and his computer displays two inappropriate pop-ups when he is searching for his topic.

   ❑ SAFE   ❑ UNSAFE

7. Laura is typing an assignment for social studies class and puts her name and date at the top.

   ❑ SAFE   ❑ UNSAFE

8. Billy is playing Internet chess on the computer with someone he does not know who lives in a different state. He chooses not to send messages back and forth with them.

   ❑ SAFE   ❑ UNSAFE

9. Carol has a blog and writes interesting information about herself. She includes information about her plans for the weekend.

   ❑ SAFE   ❑ UNSAFE

10. Nick shares his friends e-mail addresses with his brother's college friends.

    ❑ SAFE   ❑ UNSAFE

QUEST Program II UPDATE!

Dear Parent,

This week your child has been working hard in QUEST to master the skill of

Internet and E-mail Safety

Together we have learned:

- Why schools and parents have computer safety rules.

- What "personal information" is and why it is dangerous to share this information with others on the computer.

- What to do if an inappropriate or violent web page or pop up is displayed at home or at school.

- How to respond when peers suggest looking at an inappropriate or violent web page.

- How social media and other personal and video journals can be dangerous if students do not use appropriate safeguards.

You can help your child learn more at home by:

- Discussing your own home computer safety rules, especially regarding personal information, video journals, and diaries.

- Discussing safe ways to react if your child comes across an inappropriate or violent web page.

- Reviewing what "personal information" is and talking to your child about why it is dangerous to share this information with others on the computer.

e.g.: "What would you do if you were on the computer and something inappropriate appeared on the screen?"; "If you were searching for information on the computer and a web page asked you to type in your name, phone number or e-mail address, would you do it?"; "Why is that not a good idea?"

Thanks for your help!

Driving with Friends – Experiential Story

Middle and high school students are starting to think about learning how to drive. All middle school students and some high school students still need an adult to drive them from place to place. Many students take driver's training in high school and practice driving with their parents. Other students might wait to learn how to drive until they graduate from high school if they prefer. It is up to parents and students to decide when a student will learn how to drive.

Sometimes in high school a student's friends will drive before they have learned how. Students learn how to drive and get their driver's licenses at different times. Usually friends will not be allowed to have other students in the car while they are learning to drive. Students learn to drive by taking classes and practicing with their parents. Once a student has his driver's license, he can drive without a parent in the car.

Driving is one way students can be more independent, but students must also be very responsible when they drive. Students also need to be responsible when they are a passenger traveling in a car with a friend, parent, or family member. Drivers of a car must pay attention to many things in order to be safe.

When students are passengers in a car, they should always wear a seat belt even if other students want to squeeze too many students in a car, or they say it is OK not to wear a seat belt. Not wearing a seat belt can be unsafe. If there is not a seat belt, or if there are too many people trying to fit in a car, students should not accept a ride in the car. It is safer to call a parent or another family member to make arrangements for another ride home.

Students also need to remember to not distract the driver by playing loud music on the radio, making loud noises, sharing food or beverages, touching him or her, or moving around too much. Drivers of any car should be keeping their attention on the road, other cars, street signs, and lights.

Once in a while, students drink alcohol before they try to drive a car. Drinking alcohol is illegal for people under age 21. Drinking alcohol and driving at any age is against the law. Students should never get into a car if the person driving has been drinking alcohol. This is another time when students should not accept a ride in the car.

Learning how to drive a car can be fun and can make students feel more independent. Driving is also a responsibility. If students drive safely they can enjoy being independent. If students do not drive safely, parents, police officers, or judges can take away driving privileges.

Driving a car is something responsible teenagers and adults may learn to do. Parents decide when their children will learn how to drive. I can learn how to drive when my parents say it is OK. I can learn how to be a safe and responsible driver and passenger. When I'm in the car with friends, family members or parents, I can be a safe passenger by wearing my seat belt and not distracting the driver.

Driving with Friends – Activity Sheet

Materials

- ❑ "Driving with Friends" experiential story
- ❑ Driving with Friends true/false handout

Procedure

- ❑ Read "Driving with Friends" experiential story.
- ❑ Give each student a Driving with Friends true/false handout.
- ❑ Ask students to complete handout.
- ❑ Discuss.

QUEST Program II: Social Skills Curriculum for Middle School Students with Autism
© by JoEllen Cumpata and Susan Fell. Future Horizons, Inc.

Driving with Friends

Read each statement below and decide if it is true or false. Check your answer.

1. All students learn to drive when they are in high school.

    ❑ TRUE   ❑ FALSE

2. Certain cars do not require seat belt use.

    ❑ TRUE   ❑ FALSE

3. Adults and students should never drink alcohol before driving a car.

    ❑ TRUE   ❑ FALSE

4. One way students can be more independent is by learning how to drive a car.

    ❑ TRUE   ❑ FALSE

5. Loud music, food or beverages, or passengers moving around a lot or touching the driver can all be dangerous distractions to a new driver.

    ❑ TRUE   ❑ FALSE

6. It is OK to seat fifteen people in a car if they can squeeze in, as long as they can share seatbelts or sit on laps.

    ❑ TRUE   ❑ FALSE

7. Parents and students should discuss the responsibility involved in driving and decide when a student is ready to take a driver's education class.

    ❑ TRUE   ❑ FALSE

8. Most students practice driving with their parents after they have taken a driver's education class.

    ❑ TRUE   ❑ FALSE

9. It is OK to let friends ride in your car when you are learning how to drive

    ❑ TRUE   ❑ FALSE

10. Driving is a privilege that can be taken away by parents, police officers, or judges.

    ❑ TRUE   ❑ FALSE

QUEST Program II: Social Skills Curriculum for Middle School Students with Autism
© by JoEllen Cumpata and Susan Fell. Future Horizons, Inc.

QUEST Program II UPDATE!

Dear Parent,

This week your child has been working hard in QUEST Program II to master the skill of

Driving Safely with Friends

Together we have learned:

- Why some students drive in high school and others don't.

- That it is important for parents and students to decide together when driver's training will begin.

- Why seat belts are a must when driving with others.

- Why students should never drive with someone who has been drinking alcohol.

You can help your child learn more at home by:

- Discussing your own family seat-belt safety rules.

- Discussing the responsibility that goes along with taking drivers' training.

- Helping your child learn, through role-play, ways to safely exit a potentially dangerous peer-driving situation, e.g., "What would you do if you saw one of your friends drinking a beer and that friend was going to drive you home?" or "What would you do if you got in a friend's car and there were no seat belts?"

Thanks for your help!

Drugs, Alcohol, and Dangerous Behavior – Experiential Story

Middle and high school students like to relax and have fun. Many students enjoy sports, computers, games, and hobbies. Some students like to get together after school, on weekends, and during school breaks, and have fun. Usually students make good choices about the types of activities they take part in. Sometimes students make poor choices, and smoke cigarettes, try illegal drugs, or drink alcohol when they are trying to relax or have fun.

Smoking cigarettes, using illegal drugs, and drinking alcohol are not safe choices for students. Some students smoke cigarettes or marijuana or drink beer or other alcoholic beverages. Students might even try other kinds of drugs. These things are illegal. Drugs like marijuana are dangerous because they are made of plants with chemicals that change the way the brain works. Cigarettes can harm lungs and cause cancer. Students who use drugs or alcohol may not have the ability to make good decisions for themselves.

Students often make a personal decision that they will make good choices and not smoke cigarettes, use illegal drugs, or drink alcohol. Once in a while students may see other students trying these things. Students usually try these types of things at parties, in their cars, or outside. If a student sees someone doing these things, they should walk away and find a safe way to get home. Calling a parent is a good choice if a student is at a party or another social event where people are drinking alcohol or smoking marijuana.

It is a good idea for students to practice saying no to people who offer them alcohol, cigarettes, or illegal drugs. Sometimes friends will start to use these things because they don't think they are harmful. Sometimes friends use these things to look cool. When our friends want us to try illegal drugs, cigarettes, or alcohol, it is called peer pressure. If friends offer a student a cigarette, marijuana, or alcohol it is best to say, "No!" and walk away. Students do not need to explain why they don't want to do these dangerous things; they can just say no and walk away. This is a good way to be safe.

Talking with parents about illegal drugs, cigarettes, and alcohol is also a good idea. Students can talk with their parents to find out more about why these things are harmful. Students and parents can also practice ways to say no if they see friends using drugs or alcohol. Parents can also help students decide if they have made good choices for friends, and even how to tell someone they no longer want to be friends if bad choices are being made.

I can be safe when I talk with my parents about drugs, cigarettes, and alcohol, and practice saying no to friends who offer these things to me. I can also be safe when I don't smoke cigarettes, don't use illegal drugs, or avoid drinking alcohol. If I see other students doing these things at parties or other places, I can find a safe way home, or call a parent or family member.

Drugs, Alcohol, and Dangerous Behavior – Activity Sheet

Materials

- ❏ "Drugs, Alcohol, and Dangerous Behavior" experiential story
- ❏ Drugs, Alcohol, and Dangerous Behavior poster
- ❏ Drugs, Alcohol, and Dangerous Behavior scenario cards
- ❏ Sticky poster tack

Procedure

- ❏ Read "Drugs, Alcohol, and Dangerous Behavior" experiential story.
- ❏ Display Drugs, Alcohol, and Dangerous Behavior poster.
- ❏ Spread Drugs, Alcohol, and Dangerous Behavior scenario cards face down on the table.
- ❏ Ask each student to choose a card, read it aloud, and determine if the scenario describes a good or poor choice.
- ❏ Ask students to place a card in the correct box on Drugs, Alcohol, and Dangerous Behavior poster using sticky tack.
- ❏ Discuss.

Drugs, Alcohol, and Dangerous Behavior poster

Directions: Enlarge and paste on poster board.

Drugs, Alcohol, and Dangerous Behavior scenario cards

Directions: Copy on colored paper, laminate, and cut into cards.

Drugs, Alcohol, and Dangerous Behavior:
What will you choose?

Good Choice - These choices will keep you safe.

Bad Choice - These choices could put you in danger.

QUEST Program II: Social Skills Curriculum for Middle School Students with Autism
© by JoEllen Cumpata and Susan Fell. Future Horizons, Inc.

Keeping your friend's drug and alcohol use a secret from your parents.

Talking with your parents about a friend's drug or alcohol use.

Staying at a party when you notice some of the kids are drinking beer.

Leaving a party when you notice some of the kids are drinking beer.

Going into a drugstore with your friends after they tell you they plan to take cans of pop without paying for them.

Walking home when your friends tell you they are going to take cans of pop from a drugstore without paying for them.

Taking a puff off a cigarette your best friend gives you.

Refusing to take a puff from a cigarette your best friend gives you.

Trying not to think about what might happen if you see someone using drugs or drinking alcohol at a party.

Making a personal decision that you will not use illegal drugs, smoke cigarettes, or drink alcohol.

Choosing friends who drink alcohol or use illegal drugs.

Choosing friends who do not drink alcohol or use illegal drugs.

Having one sip of beer when a friend offers it to you.

Saying "no" when a friend offers you a sip of beer.

Pressuring your friends to drink alcohol, smoke cigarettes, or use illegal drugs.

Pressuring your friends not to drink alcohol, smoke cigarettes, or use illegal drugs.

QUEST Program II: Social Skills Curriculum for Middle School Students with Autism
© by JoEllen Cumpata and Susan Fell. Future Horizons, Inc.

Getting into a car when you know the driver has been drinking alcohol.

Finding a different way home when you know the driver has been drinking alcohol.

Having no interest in the most current research about illegal drugs and alcohol.

Doing computer research to learn more about the effect of illegal drugs and alcohol.

Trying dangerous activities because other students say they are fun.

Avoiding dangerous activities, even if other students say they are fun.

Telling your parents you know how to say "no" to peer pressure, even if you don't.

Practicing ways to say "no" to peer pressure with your parents.

QUEST Program II UPDATE!

Dear Parent,

This week your child has been working hard in QUEST Program II to master the skill of

Resisting Drugs, Alcohol and Dangerous Behavior

Together we have learned:

- Why some students may try drugs, alcohol, and other dangerous behaviors.

- How students can make good choices regarding drugs, alcohol, and other dangerous behaviors.

- The importance of regular family discussion regarding these topics.

- How students can influence their exposure to these behaviors by making good choices of friends.

You can help your child learn more at home by:

- Discussing your own family rules regarding parties and other peer social events.

- Researching issues with your child using the internet, books, and appropriate television opportunities.

- Discussing the Safety Contract (attached) with your child, and making a commitment to personal safety for you and your child.

- Helping your child learn through role-play ways to safely exit potentially dangerous peer substance use situations, e.g., "What would you do if a group of your friends found a pack of cigarettes?" or "How would you say no if a friend offered you a beer at the picnic today?"or "I noticed that boy on the TV show today tried some marijuana even though he really didn't want to. How could he have gotten out of that situation?"

Thanks for your help!

Safety Contract

We the _____ family, promise to keep the lines of communication open about drugs and alcohol, seat-belt use, and traffic safety. We agree to ask questions and share information regularly to ensure our safety and the safety of our friends and family.

Young Adult

I agree to always wear my seat belt when I am in a vehicle. I understand that the legal drinking age is 21. I have discussed with you and realize the dangers of drinking alcohol, using illegal substances, and driving with someone who is under the influence of drugs or alcohol. I agree to contact you if I ever find myself in a position where I believe my safety is in danger, or if I believe that the substance-use of others impacts my ability to get home safely.

_____

Signature

Parent

Should you call me, I agree to arrange for your safe transportation home, regardless of the time or circumstances. I further promise to remain calm when dealing with your situation, and to discuss it with you at a time when we can both be calm and plan for your future safety.

I agree to always wear my seat belt when I am in a vehicle. I also agree to seek safe, sober transportation home if I am ever in a situation where I have had too much to drink or a friend of mine who is driving me has had too much to drink.

_____

Signature

QUEST Program II Unit Five - Personal Safety
Unit Evaluation

Student Name _____ Date _____

Evaluator _____

We have just completed a unit in QUEST Program II on Personal Safety. Please fill out the rating scale below to assist us in determining how well your student has generalized the skills taught, and if you have noticed improvement in their level of skill over the past six weeks. Check all boxes which apply below.

O=Often S=Sometimes N=Never I=Improvement   **How Often Skill Is Observed**

Skill	O	S	N	I
Understanding how to be safe when home alone. Consistently uses family safety rules. Understands who to call when questions arise. Uses appliances, television, and computer responsibly.				
Recognizing when 911 is used. Knows by heart, or knows location of important family and friends' phone numbers. Understands the difference between a life-threatening emergency and something that can wait for a parent's return.				
Acknowledging appropriate smoke and fire safety practices. Can discuss what he/she would do if the smoke detector sounded. Understands the safe response to a small house fire. Knows when to leave a home prior to calling 911.				
Understanding the strategies to use if separated from a group in a public place. Knows to wait five to ten minutes for the group to return. Knows how to solicit assistance from appropriate adults. Knows how to recognize helpful adults – store personnel, security staff, business employees.				
Recognizing the dangers inherent to computer usage and utilizing appropriate safeguards. Understands what personal information is and why it is not shared over the internet. Refrains from seeking out inappropriate websites, e-mails or personal Web pages. Seeks adult assistance when unsure about the safety of a computer issue.				

O-Often S=Sometimes N=Never I=Improvement   **How Often Skill Is Observed**

Skill	O	S	N	I
Following safety rules when driving as a passenger or driver of a vehicle. Uses seatbelts regularly. Refrains from distracting the driver with music, movement, or touch. Recognizes the dangers of drinking and driving and can discuss strategies he/she would use if faced with this situation.				
Practicing safe behaviors regarding substance-use and risky peer behavior. Is educated regarding the dangers of cigarettes, alcohol, and illegal drugs. Discusses response behaviors to peers using drugs or alcohol with adults. Has developed a safety plan with parents for responding to dangerous peer situations.				

Comments_____

_____

Thank you for your input!

Unit 6

Vocational Readiness

Goal

To develop and improve employability skills

Objectives

➤ To learn about personal interests and related occupational clusters.

➤ To understand the relationship between employer and employee, and the value of work.

➤ To develop a flier that relates to interest areas, and practice successful ways to advertise and interview for jobs in the neighborhood.

➤ To learn how to accept redirection, suggestions, and compliments from an employer

Experiential Stories, Activities, and Parent Updates

Stories can be read by parents, teachers or students. Often students gain a deeper understanding of skills when stories can be discussed in detail in a group setting. Asking students to summarize paragraphs, relate their personal experiences, and complete activities are all effective ways to increase generalization of skills. Parent Updates provide additional ways to continue learning at home. The letter "A" denotes advanced sections appropriate for students in their second or third year of the program.

Topics included in this unit are:

1. My Skills and Interests - A

2. Working for Others - A

3. Creating a Flier and Applying for a Summer Job - A

4. Accepting Suggestions and Compliments
   from My Employer - A

My Skills and Interests – Experiential Story

Students have many skills and interests. Some students enjoy math, English, or social studies. Other students enjoy caring for animals, sports, art activities, or exploring nature. Using special skills and participating in activities that are interesting make life more fun and challenging.

Many middle and high school students are not sure what their strenghts and weaknesses are. Some students don't really think they have any special skills or interests. This is normal because most students have not had opportunities to learn about their interests or work in different jobs. Sometimes students are required to take school subjects that they find boring. We all must do things from time to time that are required of us, even if they don't interest us.

Students who know their likes and dislikes often find jobs that are fun and interesting. When students get older they may have opportunities to make money by working. Students who are not sure about their likes and dislikes are often not sure of what type of job they might like.

One way students can learn more about their likes and dislikes is to volunteer for jobs around their neighborhood. Some people even pay students to do small jobs around their homes. Another way students can learn more about their interests is by completing an Interest Inventory.

Interest inventories have been developed by psychologists, scientists, and researchers to help people learn more about themselves. Interest inventories usually ask students to decide if they would like or would not like certain activities. Students can add up their score on an inventory to find out what type of job they might like to try.

Learning about my likes and dislikes can help me find a job I really enjoy. I can complete an Interest Inventory to get more information about my skills and interests. Someday I can find a job I really enjoy.

QUEST Program II: Social Skills Curriculum for Middle School Students with Autism
© by JoEllen Cumpata and Susan Fell. Future Horizons, Inc.

My Skills and Interests – Activity Sheet

Materials

- ❑ "My Skills and Interests" experiential story
- ❑ Interest Inventory handouts
- ❑ Interest Inventory Key handouts
- ❑ Interest Inventory Summary handouts
- ❑ Pencils

Procedure

- ❑ Read "My Skills and Interests" experiential story.
- ❑ Pass out Interest Inventory handouts.
- ❑ Stress to students that there are no right or wrong answers on the Interest Inventory.
- ❑ Ask students to put a check mark next to any activity they believe they would enjoy.
- ❑ Ask students to total scores using Interest Inventory Key handouts.
- ❑ Ask students to use Interest Inventory Summary handouts to consider skills, interests and ways students can get additional experience.
- ❑ Ask students to share their top area of interest with the group.
- ❑ Discuss.

Interest Inventory

Think about the activities below. Decide if you think you might like to do the activity or if you would not like doing the activity. Place a check mark in the box next to the activities you think you would like to do.

❑   1. Plant flowers in a garden.

❑   2. Sit and put a puzzle together.

❑   3. Help older people do their grocery shopping.

❑   4. Push someone around a shopping mall in a wheelchair.

❑   5. Build a castle out of sand or building blocks.

❑   6. Wash and brush dogs.

❑   7. Wipe down tables in the cafeteria.

❑   8. Rake leaves in a park.

❑   9. Fold letters and put them in envelopes.

❑ 10. Stack cereal boxes in a grocery store.

❑ 11. Help preschool children on the playground.

❑ 12. Make copies on a copy machine.

❑ 13. Count pennies and put them into coin wrappers.

❑ 14. Put canned goods in boxes for shipping.

❑ 15. Water plants in an office.

❑ 16. Update information in computer files.

❑ 17. Fill up containers of food in a restaurant salad bar.

QUEST Program II: Social Skills Curriculum for Middle School Students with Autism
© by JoEllen Cumpata and Susan Fell. Future Horizons, Inc.

❑ 18. Walk dogs.

❑ 19. Help a student in a wheelchair eat their lunch.

❑ 20. Put pictures in picture frames.

❑ 21. Take shoes out of boxes and put them on shelves in a shoe store.

❑ 22. Fold towels for a hotel.

❑ 23. Design a computer Web page.

❑ 24. Count pencils in groups of twelve and put them into boxes.

❑ 25. Empty trash cans at a state park.

❑ 26. Take books to patients in a hospital.

❑ 27. Deliver mail to offices in a large office building.

❑ 28. Bag groceries in a grocery store.

❑ 29. Volunteer your time for the Special Olympics.

❑ 30. Clean cages and feed animals for a veterinarian.

Interest Inventory Key

Instructions: After completing the Interest Inventory, find your top three career clusters by circling the activities that were checked, and counting the total circled. The top three totals are your top career choices.

Technical Career Cluster

Activities: 2, 5, 13, 14, 20, 24   Total: _____

People working in the technical field usually work in factories, repair shops, or even out of their homes. Jobs in this cluster include; packaging, assembly, minor repair or maintenance of toys or recreational equipment, like bikes or small appliances.

Customer Service Career Cluster

Activities: 7, 10, 17, 21, 22, 28   Total: _____

People working in the customer service field usually work in restaurants, bakeries, shopping malls, or stores. Jobs in this cluster include waiter or waitress, busing tables in a restaurant, grocery store clerk or bagger, or retail stock clerk or cashier.

Business Service Career Cluster

Activities: 9, 12, 15, 16, 23, 27   Total: _____

People working in the business field usually work in a small business, office, library, or bank. Jobs in this cluster include computer data entry, mail delivery, reshelving books, office assistant, copy room assistant, or receptionist.

QUEST Program II: Social Skills Curriculum for Middle School Students with Autism
© by JoEllen Cumpata and Susan Fell. Future Horizons, Inc.

Environmental/Animal Service Career Cluster

Activities: 1, 6, 8, 18, 25, 30   Total: _____

People working in the environmental and animal service field usually work outside. Jobs in this cluster include any work with plants or animals such as park or yard maintenance, veterinary assistant, horse groomer, gardener's assistant, lawn maintenance, or florist.

Social Service Career Cluster

Activities: 3, 4, 11, 19, 26, 29   Total: _____

People working in the social service field usually work in a hospital, school or day care center, or in a retirement community. Jobs in this cluster include nurse's aide, childcare assistant, hospital aide, and senior citizen center assistant.

Interest Inventory Summary

_____   _____
Student Name   Date

Add your Interest Inventory scores and check your top three career clusters below.

❑ Technical Career Cluster

❑ Customer Service Career Cluster

❑ Business Service Career Cluster

❑ Environmental/Animal Service Career Cluster

❑ Social Service Career Cluster

List three things you enjoy doing at home, in school with friends, or other groups that use the skill cluster you circled above.

1. _____

2. _____

3. _____

List three things you can do around your home or in your community to help you get experience and prepare for a job in one of the areas above.

1. _____

2. _____

3. _____

QUEST Program II UPDATE!

Dear Parent,

This week your child has been working hard in QUEST Program II learning about

Skills and Interests

Together we have learned:

- Why it is important to develop personal interests.

- Ways personal interests relate to career clusters and future employment opportunities.

- Types of volunteer, community, and family jobs that can help students develop personal interests.

You can help your child learn more at home by:

- Talking about the personal interests you enjoy.

- Asking your child about the "Interest Inventory" they took in QUEST Program II.

- Suggest ways your child can explore their interest, e.g., "I really noticed you spent a lot of time brushing Aunt Jen's dog today. Maybe you would like to get a book on pet care?" or "I saw you looking at all the flowers at the store today. Would you like to help me plant them?" or "You seem to really enjoy drawing. Maybe you and Patty could put a comic strip together?"

Thanks for your help!

Working for Others – Experiential Story

Once in a while middle and high school students purchase items for themselves. Some students enjoy buying their own clothing or CDs. Others like purchasing books, games, or other recreational items. Students also enjoy having fun with friends by going to movies, out for ice cream, bowling, or enjoying other social activities. Many of these things cost money.

Some students can ask their parents for money for these items. Most parents cannot afford to buy everything their children want. Often students start to think that it would be wonderful if they could make some money of their own to spend on things they like. This is one way to become more independent.

Working for others is a good way to get experience and start making some spending money. Most businesses in the community hire students who are at least sixteen years old. Students who are not yet sixteen can do work for neighbors, family members, or relatives.

Students can do many things in their community as a volunteer or to make money. There are many jobs that middle and high school students can do. They include pet-sitting, dog-walking, gardening, washing windows or cars, sorting and folding laundry, helping people put groceries away, watering house plants, taking out trash, and stacking newspapers. Once students turn sixteen, they can also work in restaurants, stores, and other businesses as cashiers, baggers, computer operators, receptionists, sales people, and many other types of jobs.

When students know what they are interested in or what they like to do they can let family members and friends know that they are available to work. One way students can advertise their service is by creating a flier. Fliers let family members, friends, and neighbors know:

- What kind of work the student does.
- When they are available to do it.
- How much they charge for their service.
- Who the student is and how to reach them.

It is best if students talk with their parents about working in the neighborhood before they give out fliers. Students and parents can agree who should get a flier, how much the student should charge for their service, and how often they should work.

When students accept a job with a neighbor or family member, it is important that they get to the job on time, ask questions if they are unsure how to do the job, and do their best. This is a good way to make some spending money and get more jobs.

I can decide what jobs I can do in my community. I will talk with my parents and create my own flier. I can earn money, so that I can buy things I like and get employment experiences in my neighborhood.

QUEST Program II: Social Skills Curriculum for Middle School Students with Autism
© by JoEllen Cumpata and Susan Fell. Future Horizons, Inc.

Working for Others – Activity Sheet

Materials

- ❑ "Working for Others" experiential story
- ❑ Interest Inventory Summary handouts
- ❑ Occupational Cluster Icon cards
- ❑ Student/Parent Summer Job Questionnaire handouts
- ❑ Pencils

Procedure

- ❑ Read "Working for Others" experiential story.
- ❑ Ask students to review their Interest Inventory Summary handouts.
- ❑ Present the Occupational Cluster Icon cards one at a time and discuss possible job opportunities in the community.
- ❑ Distribute Student/Parent Summer Job Questionnaire handouts.
- ❑ Ask student to list their top three occupational clusters on question number "1" of the handout.
- ❑ Ask students to take Student/Parent Summer Job Questionnaire handouts home and discuss them with their parent.
- ❑ Ask students to complete handouts at home and bring for next class.

Occupational Cluster Icon cards

Directions: Enlarge, copy on colored paper, and cut into cards.

Technical Career Cluster

People working in the technical field usually work in factories, repair shops, or even out of their homes. Jobs in this cluster include packaging, assembly, minor repair or maintenance of toys or recreational equipment, like bikes or small appliances.

Customer Service Career Cluster

People working in the customer service field usually work in restaurants, bakeries, shopping malls, or stores. Jobs in this cluster include waiter or waitress, busing tables in a restaurant, grocery store clerk or bagger, or retail stock clerk or cashier.

QUEST Program II: Social Skills Curriculum for Middle School Students with Autism
© by JoEllen Cumpata and Susan Fell. Future Horizons, Inc.

Business Service Career Cluster

People working in the business field usually work in a small business, office, library, or bank. Jobs in this cluster include computer data entry, mail delivery, reshelving books, office assistant, copy room assistant, or receptionist.

Environmental/Animal Service Career Cluster

People working in the environmental and animal service field usually work outside. Jobs in this cluster include any work with plants or animals, such as park or yard maintenance, veterinary assistant, horse groomer, gardener's assistant, lawn maintenance, or florist.

Social Service Career Cluster

People working in the Social Service field usually work in a hospital, school, day-care center, or in a retirement community. Jobs in this cluster include nurse's aide, childcare assistant, hospital aide, and senior citizen center assistant.

Student/Parent Summer Job Questionnaire

Student Name _____   Date _____

1. The occupational clusters that matched my interests were:

    _____

    _____

    _____

2. Some jobs I can do in my neighborhood or for family members this summer are:

    _____

    _____

    _____

3. I think I should charge _____ per hour.

4. The people who should get a copy of my flier are:

    _____

    _____

    _____

QUEST Program II UPDATE!

Dear Parent,

This week your child has been working hard in QUEST Program II to master the skill of

Working for Others

Together we have learned:

- Why students benefit by working for others.

- What jobs students are typically able to do for family members or neighbors.

- How a flier can be a useful tool to let family members and neighbors know students are available to work.

You can help your child learn more at home by:

- Asking your child to discuss the flier they will be developing in QUEST Program II next class.

- Discussing the possibility of a summer job with your child.

- Informing family members, friends, and neighbors that your child will be contacting them regarding their summer job.

IMPORTANT NOTE – PLEASE DO NOT ALLOW YOUR CHILD TO DISTRIBUTE FLIERS WITH-OUT YOUR KNOWLEDGE OR TO PEOPLE YOU HAVE NOT PREVIOUSLY CONTACTED. IT IS NOT SAFE FOR STUDENTS TO GO DOOR-TO-DOOR OR TO WORK FOR STRANGERS.

Thanks for your help!

QUEST Program II: Social Skills Curriculum for Middle School Students with Autism
© by JoEllen Cumpata and Susan Fell. Future Horizons, Inc.

Creating a Flier and Applying for a Summer Job – Experiential Story

Some middle and high school students are interested in gaining job experience and making money. Usually employers prefer to hire students who are sixteen years old or older for jobs in stores or restaurants. Students who are not yet sixteen can often do odd jobs in their community to get experience and make money. Getting job experience and making money make students more independent.

Creating a flier is one way students can advertise their skills. After students create a flier they usually talk with their parents to determine who should get a copy of their flyer. It is very important that students only give fliers to people they and their parents know very well. It is not safe to give personal information to strangers, or work in a stranger's home or on their property.

When students pass out their fliers to people they know, they can take some time to apply for the job. This means that students should be ready to talk with people about what they will do, how much they will charge, and when they are available to do work. This information is usually written on student's fliers, but the best way to get hired is to be friendly and happy to talk about your job skills and the details of your possible employment.

There are four things students can do to improve their chances of getting a job. Students who really want to get hired should:

- Use good eye contact.

- Stand up straight and use appropriate body language.

- Provide information and answer questions thoroughly.

- Be enthusiastic.

Most employers, neighbors and friends appreciate it when students take the time to practice these skills. Students who are prepared to apply for jobs usually get hired.

I can practice skills I will need to apply for a job. I will try to be prepared and excited about working for others in my community. This summer I will practice what I might say to neighbors, friends, or employers before I try to get a job. I will use good eye contact and provide information in an enthusiastic way. I can also make a flier to describe my skills and the details about a job I would like. When I make a flier, practice, and ask for a job, I can get experience and also make a little money. This is one way I can become more independent.

Applying for a Summer Job – Activity Sheet

Materials

- ❏ "Creating a Flier and Applying for a Summer Job" experiential story
- ❏ Applying for a Summer Job rating sheet handouts
- ❏ Applying for a Summer Job cards
- ❏ Wet-erase markers
- ❏ Tissue or wet wipes

Procedure

- ❏ Read "Creating a Flier and Applying for a Summer Job" experiential story.
- ❏ Pass out Applying for a Summer Job rating sheet handouts.
- ❏ Explain to the students that they will be role-playing ways to apply for a summer job.
- ❏ Explain that students will rate each other using the Applying for a Summer Job rating sheet handout.
- ❏ Lay Applying for a Summer Job cards upside-down on a table.
- ❏ Ask students to choose a card and read aloud.
- ❏ Ask group what type of skills would be required for the job on the card. Also discuss what pay might be appropriate.
- ❏ Ask the student to role-play asking for the job on the card. Facilitator takes the role of employer.
- ❏ Ask students to rate the role-play.
- ❏ Share ratings.
- ❏ Discuss ways student could improve and what student did well.

Applying for a Summer Job rating sheet

Directions: Copy and laminate.

Applying for a Summer Job cards

Directions: Copy on colored paper, laminate, and cut into cards.

Applying for a Summer Job

_____   _____
Student Name   Date

Students can practice skills that help them get hired. Watch the students as they apply for a job and rate them on their skills.

Eye Contact – Is the student looking at the eyes of the employer?

❑ Well Done!   ❑ Needs Improvement

Body Language – Is the student standing up tall, keeping their arms and legs still, and facing the employer?

❑ Well Done!   ❑ Needs Improvement

Communication – Is the student giving information, answering questions, and playing verbal "ping pong" with the employer?

❑ Well Done!   ❑ Needs Improvement

Enthusiasm – Is the student smiling and excited about the job?

❑ Well Done!   ❑ Needs Improvement

A neighbor has several dogs who need walking daily.

Your mother says your grandmother needs help weeding her garden.

Your neighbor needs a babysitter for three children.

The store on the corner has a sign in the window for grocery delivery help.

One of the teachers at school asks for students to help make copies.

Your uncle says he knows several friends who need their cars washed.

You want to start a yard work business in your neighborhood.

You want to start a pet-sitting business in your neighborhood.

QUEST Program II: Social Skills Curriculum for Middle School Students with Autism
© by JoEllen Cumpata and Susan Fell. Future Horizons, Inc.

Your father says his boss is looking for someone to work in the mailroom.

Your mother tells you the pet store down the street needs someone to walk the dogs.

Your elderly neighbor needs help with her grocery shopping.

Your aunt asks if you would be interested in doing some house painting.

Your elderly neighbor just bought a computer and needs help learning how to send e-mail.

A neighbor has a cat and is going out of town. She needs someone to feed her pet while she is gone.

A neighbor is going on a vacation and is looking for someone to water the lawn while he is gone.

Your grandfather needs help mowing his lawn.

Creating a Flier – Activity Sheet

Materials

- ❑ "Creating a Flier and Applying for a Summer Job" experiential story
- ❑ Completed Interest Inventory Summary handouts
- ❑ Sample fliers
- ❑ Computers
- ❑ Paper
- ❑ Pencils

Procedure

- ❑ Read "Creating a Flier and Applying for a Summer Job" experiential story.
- ❑ Using completed Interest Inventory Summary handouts, ask students to create flier for a summer job.
- ❑ Share fliers with the group.
- ❑ Copy fliers on colored paper.
- ❑ Provide each student with several copies of their flier.
- ❑ Discuss who students might solicit regarding employment.

SPECIAL NOTE: Contact all parents prior to initiating this activity to ensure that they support summer employment. Parent Update indicates parents and students must agree upon friendly neighbors, family members, and friends prior to handing out our fliers.

Ryan's Pet Sitting Service

Will feed and walk your pets while you are away.

$3.00 per day

Call Ryan at 123-4567

Emily's Plant Watering Service

Will water plants inside or outside of your home.

$2.00 day

Call Emily at 123-4567

Larry's Odd Job Service

- Gardening
- Yard Work
- Digging Holes

$2.00 - $6.00
per job
for laying
topsoil

Available weekends

Call Larry at 123-4567

QUEST Program II UPDATE!

Dear Parent,

This week your child has been working hard in QUEST Program II to master the skill of

Creating a Flier and Applying for a Summer Job

Together we have learned:

- How to create a flier to let family members and neighbors know students are available to work.

- How to propose employment with family members or neighbors.

You can help your child learn more at home by:

- Practicing with your child before they discuss summer employment with family members, friends, or neighbors.

- Assisting your child to distribute fliers, prepare for, and complete summer jobs.

IMPORTANT NOTE – PLEASE DO NOT ALLOW YOUR CHILD TO DISTRIBUTE FLIERS WITHOUT YOUR KNOWLEDGE OR TO PEOPLE YOU HAVE NOT PREVIOUSLY CONTACTED. IT IS NOT SAFE FOR STUDENTS TO GO DOOR-TO-DOOR OR TO WORK FOR STRANGERS.

Thanks for your help!

Accepting Suggestions and Compliments from My Employer – Experiential Story

Some middle and high school students want to gain experience, use skills they enjoy, and make some extra money. One good way to do this is to work during the summer for a neighbor, family member or friend, or for a local business.

When students work for an employer, family member, or neighbor, it is important that they understand how to do a good job. Sometimes employers will want to explain the job. Sometimes employers change their mind about how the job should be done. Once in a while employers are unhappy with the work after it is completed. It is not unusual for employers to spend time talking to people working for them.

Students need to listen when their employer talks to them. When students listen, they need to remember to look at their employer and stand about an arm's length away. If the employer is explaining the job, it is OK for the student to ask questions if they don't understand. It is also OK for students to write down things to help them remember how to do a good job.

When employers are pleased with the work that has been done it is not unusual for them to give the student a compliment. Employers might tell students that they are pleased with how well the student did the job, or with how quickly the job was completed. Students can say, "Thank you," when employers give them a compliment.

Sometimes employers are not pleased with the work. It is OK for an employer to change their mind about how they want work done, or to correct a student if they are doing the job wrong. When employers correct a student, it is important that the student listens closely, and tries to correct their mistake next time.

Good employees listen to their boss, thank them for compliments, and try to correct their mistakes. Students who are good employees will be paid well and may be asked to do more work, or even work for other employers.

I can be a good employee when I listen to my boss, thank him or her for compliments, and try to do my best. When my boss corrects me, or changes the way he or she wants something done, I can listen and do my best. I can take time to correct mistakes I make.

Accepting Suggestions and Compliments from My Employer – Activity Sheet

Materials

- ❑ "Accepting Suggestions and Compliments from My Employer" experiential story
- ❑ Employer Compliments cards
- ❑ Employer Suggestions cards

Procedure

- ❑ Read "Accepting Suggestions and Compliments from My Employer" experiential story.
- ❑ Mix Employer Suggestions and Employer Compliments cards and lay them upside-down on the table.
- ❑ Remind students they are to thank employers for compliments and listen and correct mistakes if possible when employers give suggestions.
- ❑ Ask student to choose a card.
- ❑ Ask student to respond appropriately to card.
- ❑ Discuss.

Employer Compliments cards

Directions: Copy on colored paper, laminate, and cut into cards.

Employer Suggestions cards

Directions: Copy on colored paper, laminate, and cut into cards.

QUEST Program II: Social Skills Curriculum for Middle School Students with Autism
© by JoEllen Cumpata and Susan Fell. Future Horizons, Inc.

You did a fabulous job stacking those soup cans so quickly.

I'm thrilled with the garden. You cleaned out all the weeds.

The children said they really had fun with you today at the park!

It is so nice seeing you each Thursday right on time to take out the trash.

My car is so clean, and the hose, bucket, and sponge are all clean and put away.

It is really helpful to have you here to help me put my groceries away.

You are doing a great job clearing the tables.

I'm very happy with your punctuality. Keep up the good work.

I think you may have misunderstood me. I don't want those boxes there!

Oh no! That's not the bush I wanted you to remove!

I'm not happy with the way you cut the lawn. It is much too long.

When you do gardening, I expect you to sweep the driveway afterwards.

The children said you watched TV all day. I really need them to be outside more.

You may not have operated a commercial dishwasher before. You close the door when it's on!

You spoke to that customer in a mean way. I need you to apologize to her.

I can't keep you working here if you are late again.

QUEST Program II UPDATE!

Dear Parent,

This week your child has been working hard in QUEST Program II to master the skill of

Accepting Suggestions and Compliments from an Employer

Together we have learned:

- The importance of listening and asking questions when employers are giving directions.

- How to accept a compliment from an employer.

- How to make amends when a mistake has been made.

You can help your child learn more at home by:

- Asking your child to give you eye contact and stand about an arm's length away when you are providing them with directions.

- Encouraging your child to ask questions at home when they don't understand a direction.

- Asking your child how their first employment experiences are going and providing guidance when mistakes occur, e.g., "I know you were very excited about working for Mrs. Smith. I know next time you will remember to put the hose away." or "It is important to be polite to all the customers, even the nasty ones. How about if we practice a bit before you go to work tomorrow?"

Thanks for your help!

QUEST Program II Unit Six - Vocational Readiness
Unit Evaluation

Student Name _____ Date _____

Evaluator _____

We have just completed a unit in QUEST Program II on Vocational Readiness. Please fill out the rating scale below to assist us in determining how well your student has generalized the skills taught, and if you have noticed improvement in their level of skill over the past six weeks. Check all boxes which apply below.

O=Often S=Sometimes N=Never I=Improvement   **How Often Skill Is Observed**

Skill	O	S	N	I
Understand and appreciate personal skills and interests Identify areas of interest and skill. Verbalize possible career clusters, jobs, or activities that utilize skills and interests. Discuss ways to improve current skills or learn new skills.				
Identify reasons employment is valuable Discuss and consider possible local community service, volunteer, or paid work opportunities.				
Utilize promotional strategies to secure part-time or summer employment Discuss skill sets and possible summer employment ideas with family, friends, neighbors, and local businesses. Attempt part-time, community service, or paid employment.				
Understand how to communicate appropriately with an employer Listen when job requirements and duties are discussed. Correct mistakes without arguing or becoming angry, sarcastic, or withdrawn.				

Comments_____

_____

Thank you for your input!

References

American Speech-Language-Hearing Association. (2005). Evidence-based practice in communication disorders (Position Statement).

Attwood, T. (1998). *Asperger's syndrome: A Guide for Parents and Professionals*. London: Jessica Kingsley.

Attwood, T. (2003). Frameworks for behavioral interventions. *Child and Adolescent Psychiatric Clinics of North America*, 12(1), 65-86.

Attwood, T. (2000). Strategies for improving the social integration of children with Asperger's Syndrome. *Autism*, 4(1), 85-100.

Bock, M. A. (2001). SODA strategy: Enhancing social interaction skills of youngsters with Asperger Syndrome. *Intervention in School and Clinic*, 36(5), 272-278.

Brinton, B., Robinson, L., & Fujiki, M. (2004). Description of a program for social language intervention: If you can have a conversation, you can have a relationship. *Language, Speech and Hearing Services in Schools*, 35, 283-290.

Brunner, D. & Seung, H. (2009). Evaluation of the efficacy of communication-based treatments for autism spectrum disorders: A literature review. *Communication Disorders Quarterly*, 31, 15-41.

California Department of Education, (1997). Best practices for designing and delivering programs for individuals with autism spectrum disorders. Sacramento, CA

Justice, L. & Fey, M. (2004, September 21). Evidence-Based Practice in Schools: Integrating Craft and Theory with Science and Data. *The ASHA Leader*.

Girolametto, L., Weitzmn, E, & Greenberg, J. (2004). The effects of verbal support strategies on small-group peer interactions. *Language, Speech, and Hearing Services in Schools*, 35, 254-68.

Gray, C. (2000). *The New Social Story Book*. Illustrated edition. Arlington, TX: Future Horizons.

Gresham, F. M., Sugai, G., & Horner, R. H. (2001). Interpreting outcomes of social skills training for students with high-incidence disabilities. *Exceptional Children*, 67, 331-344.

Klin, A., Sparrow, S. S., Marans, W. D., Carter, A., & Volkmar, F. R. (2000). Assessment issues in children and adolescents with Asperger Syndrome. In A. Klin, F. R. Volkmar, & S. S. Sparrow (Eds.), *Asperger Syndrome* (pp. 309-339). New York: Guilford Press.

Krasny, L., Williams, B.J., Provencal, S., & Ozonoff, S. (2003). Social skills intervention for the autism spectrum: Essential ingredients and a model curriculum. *Child & Adolescent Psychiatric Clinics of North America*, (12)1, 107-122.

Kroeger, K. A., Schultz, J.R., & Newsom, C. (2007). A comparison of two group-delivered social skills programs for young children with autism. *Journal of Autism and Developmental Disorders*, 37(5), 808-817.

Lopata, C., Thomeer, M. L., Volker, M.A., & Nida, R.E. (2006). Effectiveness of a cognitive-behavioral treatment on the social behaviors of children with Asperger disorder. *Focus on Autism and Other Developmental Disabilities*, 21(4), 237-244.

Mackay, T., Knott, F., & Dunlop, A. (2007). Developing social interaction and understanding in individuals with autism spectrum disorder: A groupwork intervention. *Journal of Intellectual and Developmental Disabilities*, 32, 279-290.

Murray, D., Ruble, L., Willis, H., & Molloy, C. (2009). Parent and teacher report of social skills in children with autism spectrum disorders. *Language, Speech, and Hearing Services in Schools*, 40, 109-115.

Myles, B. & Adreon, D. (2001). *Asperger syndrome and adolescence and practical solutions for school success*. Shawnee Mission, KS, Autism Asperger Publishing.

National Standards Project Report-Promoting Evidence-Based Practice, (2007). The National Autism Center, Randolph, MA

Rao, P., Beidel, D., & Murray, M. (2007). Social skills interventions for children with Asperger's syndrome or high-functioning autism: A review and recommendations. *Journal of Autism and Developmental Disorders*, 38, 353-361.

Ruble, L. A., Willis, H., & Crabtree, V. (2008). Social skills group therapy for autism spectrum disorders. *Journal of Clinical Case Studies*, 7, 287-300.

Rubin, E. & Laurent, A. (2004). Implementing a curriculum-based assessment to prioritize learning objectives in Asperger syndrome and high-functioning autism. *Topics in Language Disorders*, 24, 298-315.

Sansoti, F. (2010). Teaching social skills to children with autism spectrum disorders using tiers of support: A guide for school-based professionals. *Psychology in the Schools*, 47(3), 257-281.

Saulnier, C. & Klin, A. (2007). Brief report: social and communication abilities and disabilities in high functioning individuals with autism and Asperger syndrome. *Journal of Autism and Developmental Disorders*, 37, 788-793.

Stichter, J. (2010). Social competence intervention for youth with Asperger syndrome and high-functioning autism: An initial investigation. *Journal of Autism and Developmental Disorders*, (published online, February 17, 2010).

Tantam, D. (1991). Asperger syndrome in adulthood. In U. Frith (Ed.), *Autism and Asperger Syndrome*. 147–183 Cambridge, UK: Cambridge University Press.

Tse, J., Strulovitch, J., Tagalakis, B., Meng, L., & Fombonne, E. (2007). Social skills training for adolescents with Asperger syndrome and high-functioning autism. *Journal of Autism and Developmental Disorders*, (37)10, 1960-1968.

Thiemann, K., Goldstein, H. (2001). Social stories, written text cues, and video feedback: Effects on social communication of children with autism. *Journal of Applied Behavior Analysis*, 34, 425-445.

Thiemann, K. & Goldstein, H. (2004). Effects of peer training and written text cueing on social communication of school-age children with pervasive developmental disorder. *Journal of Speech, Language, and Hearing Research*, 47, 126-144.

Tsatsanis, K., Foley, C. & Donebower, C. (2004). Contemporary outcomes, research, and program goals for Asperger syndrome and high-functioning autism. *Topics in Language Disorders*, 24, 249-259.

Webb, B., Miller, S., Pierce, T., Strawser, S. & Jones, W. (2004). Effects of social skills instruction for high-functioning adolescents with autism spectrum disorders. *Focus On Autism and Other Developmental Disorders*, 19, 53-62.

Index

QUEST Program II: Social Skills Curriculum for Middle School Students with Autism
© by JoEllen Cumpata and Susan Fell. Future Horizons, Inc.

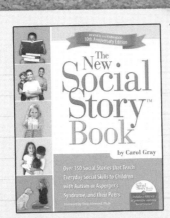
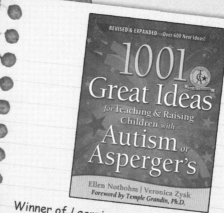